Whether or not it eventually happens, Peter Molyneux's plans for bringing *Black & White* to market involve producing two different retail versions: a 'good' version in white-hued packaging, and an 'evil' edition resplendent in more sinister tones. Those opting for the more saintly version with find themselves stumping up £5 more for the privilege; the extra cash will go to charity. Even at the point of purchase, players will begin making the kind of moral choice that forms such a fundamental part of the *Black & White* experience (see p42).

With this in mind, this historic issue of **Edge** is available in 'good' and 'evil' formats, too. (You don't have to pay extra to be a 'good' reader, you're simply getting the opportunity to make fellow Tube travellers aware of your leanings.)

Edge has produced issues with two different covers before, of course, but this month sees the appearance of something never before attempted: the definitive list of the 100 best videogames ever made (see p52). The feature was almost dropped part way through the production of the issue, so difficult was the selection process. But **Edge** staff battled on (usually against each other) and after many tortuous hours finally delivered. The results will surely be as contentious to read as they were to compile. As always, your opinions are welcome.

It wasn't only **Edge**'s top 100 that caused disagreement in the office this month. Looking back at the pieces of gaming hardware featured in 'Videogaming: the Odyssey' (see p72), another thorny mediation emerged: which of these relics was the most consequential in the development of videogaming as an entertainment form? Was it the Atari VCS? The ZX Spectrum? The NES? But this was a debate to which there was no conclusion. Whether it was the player-missile sprite capacity of the Atari 400 or the SID chip of the C64, each machine offered something to earn it equal recognition in a roll call of technology that has changed lives.

Good or evil, enjoy the issue. Here's to a new millennium filled to bursting with the most consequential videogaming kit yet.

Contacts

Editorial

Future Publishing
30 Monmouth Street
Bath, BANES, BA1 2BW

Telephone: 01225 442244
Fax: 01225 732275
Email: edge@futurenet.co.uk
Advertising and recruitment:
neil.abraham@futurenet.co.uk

Subscriptions

Future Publishing Ltd
FREEPOST BS4900, Somerton
Somerset TA11 6BR
Telephone customer services:
01458 271112
Telephone customer order line:
01458 271112
Fax: 01225 822523
Email: subs@futurenet.co.uk

People on Edge

Tony Mott editor
João Sanches deputy editor
Jon Jordan writer
Alex Morss production editor
Christophe Kagotani Tokyo bureau

Terry Stokes art editor
Darren Phillips designer

Emma Lewis advertising manager
Neil Abraham business dev manager
Amar Hussain classified advertising
Advertising fax 0171 486 5678
Marc Watson production coordinator
Lou Reffell production manager
Production fax 01225 732293
Caroline Coles ad design
Beccy Stables print services coordinator
Judith Green group production manager
Rachel Spurrier pre-press coordinator
Simon Windsor, Mark Gover,
Jason Titley colour scanning
Chris Power foreign licensing
Jackie Garford publisher
Rob Price publishing director
Jane Ingham managing director
Greg Ingham chief executive

Colour reproduction

Colourworks Repro, Bristol
Phoenix Repro, Bath

Print

Cradley Print, Warley, West Midlands
Edge is printed on Royal Press 90gsm

Production of Edge

Hardware Power Macintosh, G3, G4, i-Book,
iMac, Quadra by Apple
Software *QuarkXPress*, Adobe *Photoshop*,
Macromedia *FreeHand*,
Pixar *Typestry* and Nisus *Writer*
Typography (Adobe®)
Formata light/**regular/medium/bold**
Vectora light/**bold/black** Base12Sans/
bold/Univers Ultra Condensed
Cover Stock Keaykolour antique lustre board
300gsm
Fifth colour Pantone® 8401

Inside covers Telegraph Colour Library/Jack Newton
Special thanks Simon Chittenden (props),
Jason Moore (retro hardware), Kevan Heydon
(retro hardware), and Estate of Marcel
Duchamp/ADAGP Paris & DACS London 1999

Edge recognises all copyrights in this
issue. Where possible, we have
acknowledged the copyright holder.
Contact us if we have failed to credit your
copyright and we will be happy to correct
any oversight.

EDGE is the registered trade mark of Edge
Interactive Media Inc. Used under licence.

Future Publishing Ltd is part of The Future
Network plc.

The Future Network plc serves the information
needs of groups of people who share a passion.
We aim to satisfy their passion by creating
magazines and Web sites that offer superb value
for money, trustworthy information, multiple ways
to save time and money, and are a pleasure to
read or visit.
This simple strategy has helped create one of the
fastest-growing media companies in the world: we
publish more than 115 magazines, 20 magazine
Web sites and a number of Web networks from
offices in five countries. The company also
licenses 42 magazines in 30 countries.

The Future Network is a public company quoted
on the London Stock Exchange.

Black & White 42

Creation is in your hands. Will you make mice or monsters? **Edge** climbs
into the animal cage with Peter Molyneux and the specimens at Lionhead

The Edge Top 100 52

 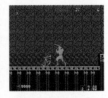

Any format, any age, any genre – there was no criterion except quality.
Discover the most illustrious titles ever to grace gamers' consciousness

PRESCREEN ALPHAS 13

On the eve of a new era, Edge identifies key forthcoming titles in an extended section

THE BOUNCER (PS2) **20**

GT2 (PS) **14**

BIOHAZARD CODE: VERONICA (DC) **21**

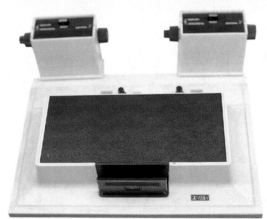

VIDEOGAMING: THE ODYSSEY 72

Edge trawls through hardware's haphazard history

ATD 38

When **Edge** last visited, Jaguar software was the company's focus. How time changes everything

THE SIMS 32

Meeting the new breed of little computer people

Cutting Edge

Cutting Edge Cutting Edge Cutting Edge Cutting Edge Cutting Edge Cutting Edge Cutting Edge Cutting Edge Cutting Edge

The latest news from the world of interactive entertainment

MASSIVE SHAKE-UP POISED TO RELAUNCH SEGA

Reorganisation of consumer division creates ten companies in race for online supremacy and profitability

Sega is relying on innovative games with online aspects, such as *Seaman* and *Chu-Chu Rocket*, to gain new consumers and reinvent itself

Sega Enterprises has announced a massive internal shake-up as it repositions itself to join the race among big games companies to become online players.

Sega wants to capitalise on the strength of Internet stocks, by repositioning its consumer and amusement machine businesses within what it is describing as a "network entertainment kingdom."

Sega chairman **Isao Okawa** said: "I think that in the future there is the possibility of Sega becoming a software-only company. Online and networked entertainment are the future and that is how we will compete."

The reorganisation sees Sega's software R&D division

> Several new Dreamcast peripherals are expected to improve the format's online potential. These include a digital camera, microphone, cable modem and Iomega's Zip drive. Sega will start distributing online games in the spring

being split into ten separate companies. Its trouble-struck arcade operation will be relaunched as a separate entity. Four of the new companies, Sega Toys, Sega Muse, Nextec and Sega Logistics, will be floated on the stock exchange.

Sega also expects to release around ¥100bn (£600m) through the launch and floatation of Japanese and American companies. These will handle Dreamcast's e-business and online gaming.

A crucial part of the changes is the reinvention of Sega's core Dreamcast/Naomi business as an integrated broadband network. It follows Sony's recent announcement that it will be aggressively levering PlayStation2 as a set-top box for the download of games, movies and music, after the rollout of Sony's own broadband network in 2001.

Sega admits that Dreamcast has so far failed to attract sufficient new customers in Japan, despite its premature price cut. It says this is now a priority. The company expects novel games such as *Space Channel 5* and *Seaman* to make the console a success. *Seaman*, in particular, has been a surprise hit in Japan, steadily working towards sales of 250,000.

Sega will also use its new network plans to push Dreamcast's compatibility with handheld devices, such as SNK's Neo-Geo Pocket Color and its forthcoming 32bit replacement. Several Dreamcast peripherals will be released

Iomega's Dreamcast Zip drive: a crucial part of Sega's online success

(Left) Sega chairman Isao Okawa is keen to reposition the company as an online player, while vice president Sadahiko Hirose's move to At Home Japan should result in high-speed access for users

in 2000, all expected to improve the console's online potential. These include a digital camera, microphone, cable modem, and Iomega's Zip drive.

Sega's remaining arcade centres will embrace the new model, with connections via fibre optic cable. This will create a large-scale area network that home users and thirdparty content providers can access. After closing 150 loss-making sites in Japan last year, Sega hopes to open nine new arcades as well.

Sega will start distributing games online by spring 2000. More than 300 Mega Drive and PC Engine titles will be made available for download via a Dreamcast unit, using a custom GD-Rom.

Meanwhile, Sega Music Network will distribute 15,000 tracks via Dreamcast and NTT's i-Mode mobile phone network. **Sadahiko Hirose**, Sega's vice president, who was overseeing Dreamcast's online capabilities, has left the company to become president of At Home Japan, an AT&T-affiliated ISP.

The move is related to the deal CSK, Sega's parent company, recently signed with AT&T to use its cable network for high-speed Internet access. It is expected

that At Home Japan will announce improved Net access for Dreamcast users.

Big deals

December saw other big publishers refine their Internet strategies. EA signed a £50m five-year deal to provide exclusive games for AOL and access to titles such as *Ultima Online* and *Black & White*.

Other content will include chat rooms, the ability to download games, and find online opponents. It is

believed that a basic service will cost $5 per month, while unlimited access will be available for around $10. EA has also bought Kesmai, an online game developer and content provider.

Eidos has revealed more about its ambitious Internet plans, following its £34m acquisition of Maximum Holdings. This US Internet group already attracts more than 3.5m hits per month to its various game sites. Eidos will use it to enhance the distribution and marketing of its online games.

SEGA SHARES AND PROFIT

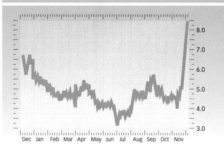

Despite posting losses of £114m in the six months to September, the latter half of 1999 has seen Sega's share price rocket from earlier record lows. In particular, financial analysts' views on the company's reorganisation plans have been positive, with several analysts contacted by Bloomberg financial services upgrading their 'sell' advice to 'buy'. Sega stock rose 77 per cent in the days following the announcement.

DREAMCAST BLUNDERS **DOWN UNDER**
Twice-delayed, trouble-struck launch sours Sega's reputation in Australia

Despite the cheery, hopeful message, Australian Dreamcast owners could have to wait until March before the console's online aspects are released

Dreamcast's future in Australia is looking bleak after what many are calling the worst console launch in videogaming history.

Launched on November 30, Australian consumers were treated to a litany of bewildering blunders.

The console's online component was unavailable due to the ISP contract only being signed the day before.

As it transpired, this wasn't so much of a problem for the $500 (£200) machine – as the promised GD-ROM demo CD enabling access was not included in the box.

A week earlier, customs officers impounded virtually the entire supply of Dreamcast launch

software due to a lack of 'country of origin' information on the packaging.

Gamers who turned up on day one, mostly wooed by *Soul Calibur,* were left feeling betrayed. Apart from no software, most retailers had no extra controllers, no VMUs, and a box displaying an empty promise of immediate Internet access.

Many of those who did manage to buy units vented their dissatisfaction through Net newsgroups, making bitter comments about the CD player sitting by their television and the hole in their bank balance. The upshot of the fiasco was clear: one large retail chain reported five console sales over the first few days, while another notched up an impressive eight.

NEW VOODOOS CAST **MULTI-CHIP SPELL**

Latest boards from 3dfx promise ultra-fast fillrate, thanks to multiple chip design

G raphics boards giant 3dfx has used the Comdex exhibition to unveil its long-awaited Napalm technology. But its new boards will not be available until the end of March.

The news comes hot on the heels of the release of boards based on rival firm Nvidia's GeForce chip, which look certain to dominate sales over Christmas. 3dfx's decision not to support hardware transform and lighting, the key feature of Nvidia's Geforce chip, demonstrates a stark contrast in approach between these fiercely competitive companies. 3dfx hopes to persuade consumers that high fillrates and smooth graphics are preferable to more polygons and effects such as cubic environment mapping.

Based on the VSA-100 (Voodoo Scableable Architecture) graphics chip, 3dfx and partner Quantum3D have designed a range of boards for gamers and high-end workstations. These range from the Voodoo 4 4500 (using one VSA-100 chip) to the $40,000 Heavy Metal GX+ CGI solutions (32 VSA-100 chips).

The latest game to demonstrate the potential of the T-buffer's motion blur effects is *Quake III: Arena*

3dfx has decided not to support hardware transform and lightning, the key feature of Nvidia's Geforce chip. This demonstrates a stark contrast in approach between these fiercely competitive companies

New 3dfx CEO Alex Leupp's promise to turn the company around relies on the future success of its VSA-100-based boards

Using 0.25-micron technology with 14m transistors per chip, each VSA-100 can support up to 64Mb of memory, using Intel's AGP 4x architecture and 32bit colour rendering. Calculating two pixels per clock cycle, it can handle 333 Mpixel per second – a figure that rises to 1.47 Gpixels in the four-chip set-up of the Voodoo 5 6000 AGP.

Returning to the Scan Line Interleave (SLI) technology which 3dfx first demonstrated with its dual Voodoo 2 board, it hopes to engineer a competitive product for each price point in the 3D graphics market. Boards will be based on one, two, four, eight, 16 and 32 VSA-100 chips.

The boards will be shipped with 32Mb of RAM per chip. The single-chip Voodoo 4 4500 AGP and PCI boards, the two-chip Voodoo 5 5500 AGP, and the four-chip Voodoo 5 6000

AGP are designated for games. The much-vaunted T-Buffer technologies (allowing full screen antialiasing and motion blur) and its open source FXT-1 texture compression are supported.

With graphic chips developing much faster than Moore's Law dictates, the biggest challenge 3dfx faces is the race to retail. Nvidia is committed to a six-month cycle, suggesting its next GeForce-based chip will surface in March. Matrox is expected to release details of its G400 successor at the Games Developer Conference, also in March. There is much speculation concerning 3dfx's next-generation Rampage chip. Boards based on Rampage are expected to ship around August.

The latest Voodoo boards (from left to right): the cheapest option will be the single-chip Voodoo 4 4500, available in AGP and PCI. With 32Mb of RAM it is set to retail at $180 (UK price TBA). The two-chip Voodoo 5 5500 AGP will cost $300, while the gigapixel-per-second Voodoo 5 6000 AGP will clock in at $600

SEGA INNOVATES AT WINTER COIN-OP SHOW

Annual Japanese trade event sees AM divisions pulling together in push towards originality

A surge in sport games, puzzlers and music titles on offer at Sega's private winter show in Tokyo indicated the company's continuing quest to attract 'light users' and female gamers into arcades.

Software R&D#2 was one of the busiest departments at the annual event, aimed at introducing arcade operators to forthcoming coin-ops.

F355 Twin still attracted plenty of interest, but the big driving game of the event was *18Wheeler* – a US-based trucking simulation. Gamers choose from four vehicles and then race through ten stages from New York to San Francisco, avoiding heavy traffic.

The handling is as heavy as you'd expect – partly due to the 48cm steering wheel – and a subwoofer in the seat provides a suitably meaty engine rumble.

R&D#2 also showed off *Virtua NBA*, a highly intuitive two-button (pass and shoot/block) sim, with all 29 leagues from the real sport. Animation and background visuals are partocularly impressive. Unsurprisingly, the game offers a link option for multiplayer games.

Multiplayer party-style games are always a good

Yu Suzuki's stripped-down *Ferrari F355 Twin* cabinets remain hot favourites with highly competitive Japanese arcade goers. Expect a UK release early in 2000. A DC conversion still appears some way off

Ferrari F355 Twin attracted plenty of interest but the big driving game of the event was *18Wheeler* – a US-based trucking simulation. Gamers chose from four vehicles and then race through ten stages

way of enticing those elusive non-hardcore gamers. Or at least that's what Software R&D 3 hopes. The team's *Mars TV* has groups of three players competing in a series of TV quiz shows on Mars. The objective is to become the most famous contestant, achieved by victory in the 15 snappy mini-games on offer.

Accompanying this was *Touch 2*, a touchscreen puzzle game based around logic problems. When you've finished the game, the machine prints out your IQ – perhaps a little too revealing for a

night at the arcade. Elsewhere, Yuji Naka was on hand to show off *Samba de Amigo*, which has just acquired a new tune – Euro hit 'Macarena'.

Toshihiro Nagoshi (*Daytona, SCUD Race*) and his Software R&D#4 dept revealed to **Edge** that his team will unveil a major game at AOU next year, as will R&D#1. R&D#5 held off the premiere of its *Model 4 Star Wars Racer* until the major coin-op show. All the games on show at this private event were Naomi titles, reinforcing Sega's commitment to the format.

(Top) *Virtua NBA* sees the franchise take on basketball, while *Mars TV* is for 'light users'

The big game of the show, in more ways than one, was R&D#2's *18Wheeler*. This behemoth of a trucking simulator even offers an appropriately sized steering wheel and forearm-busting handling

MILIA 2000 TO SHOWCASE EDGE WINNER

Cannes festival set to promote victorious entry in co-sponsored competition

E dge in partnership with Milia 2000 has launched a competition open to UK developers offering the chance to showcase a new piece of work at this year's exhibition in Cannes.

The aim of the **Edge**/Developers @Milia 2000 Competition is to select the best interactive project or application under development. Projects will be judged on originality, quality and variety of content, interactivity and navigation, graphics, video and sound quality, innnovation, and technological skills.

The prize will include a return flight and accommodation for Milia 2000, free registration, and an exhibition desk. To enter, see the competition entry form on p137 or visit the **Edge** Web site (http://fnetedit1/edge). The closing date is January 26.

To encourage creative content development, Milia has announced an expanded program of events at the show, taking place at the Palais des Festival from February 14-18.

Developers on all platforms will have the chance to present new

Milia 2000, in Cannes, will be the venue for much hobnobbing for the talented winner of the Edge/Developers@Milia2000 competition

projects, network, and visit conferences aimed at helping them to learn about aligning their work with market needs.

First-time exhibitors will have a chance to demonstrate their latest projects, for a charge of £350, at the Developer Villages.

Milia 2000 opens with a Think.Tank. Summit on February 14-15, with conferences geared to senior

executives from the interactive content industry. It is being billed as a groundbreaking event which will provide a wealth of new business opportunities.

The Milia 2000 exhibition follows on February 15-18 and will showcase creative content and companies shaping the future of interactive game development.

SNK SEEKS NAOMI ROMANCE

Latest *Fatal Fury* to be last big title on Hyper Neo-Geo 64

T he main attraction at SNK's recent private coin-op show was a new *Fatal Fury* title. Subtitled *Mark of the Wolves*, it features a whole new generation of fighters. It was originally designed as a 3D game, but SNK felt that the Hyper Neo-Geo 64 board couldn't deal with the level of graphics it hoped to create.

It is expected that this will mark the end for the technology on leading titles – SNK has now chosen Naomi as its standard platform. The game to benefit from this decision will be a new fully 3D *King of Fighters* title. It is expected to premiere at AOU.

SNK also promoted links between arcade and Neo-Geo Pocket titles and hinted that the 32bit version of its handheld will be revealed later this year.

Midway offered game demos, including the latest title in the *Beast Busters* lightgun series. *Invasion* (see Alphas) allows players to use various vehicles throughout the action. The game's visuals are significantly smoother and faster than previous outings. It also revealed *Sport Station*, a single cabinet running both *NBA Showtime* and *NFL Blitz*.

Mark of the Wolves and Midway's Invasion (above) proved draws at SNK's private show

SUNDAY EVENING 21:00

get some time together.

40 hours continuous playtime. 18 hot titles. 16bit colour power. 6 cool cases. 1 machine. Zero alternative.

NeoGeo £59.99 Games £24.99. Available at Electronics Boutique, Game, HMV, MVC, Dixons, Currys, @Jakarta, Beatties and all good independent retailers.

Watch found in launderette

All-Night-Bright Launderette, Notting Hill Gate

What was that glow under the spin dryer? Your Lorus Fusion with Vividigi display? Looks like it was suds resistant as well as water resistant. Left by man in chauffeur's uniform and woman in tiara who stripped and washed their clothes last Saturday at 2am Call Beryl on (01628) 410 371

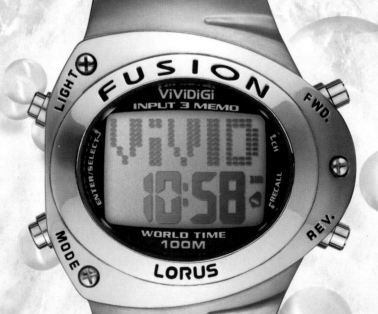

FUSION
by LORUS

PRESCREEN

EDGE PREMIERES INTERACTIVE ENTERTAINMENT'S FRESHEST FACES

Return of a medieval dilemma

It's time to remember technology is just a means to an end

A thousand years ago, the hottest question among the intelligentsia was: how many angels could dance on the head of a pin? And strange as it seems, a similar line of inquiry now appears to be stirring controversy in the development community.

Pubs around Guildford are resounding to heated debates about just how many monkeys can fit into an infinite polygon engine. There's plenty to mull over. Does the size of the monkeys count? And how is infinity defined – using traditional Euclidean geometry or DirectX texture compression on a screen resolution of 1028x768? It's enough to get anyone scratching their beard.

If only it were. The fact remains that far too much time is spent talking about the shininess of technology when the only thing that matters is how a game actually plays – something that developers such as Elixir, Lionhead and Rare freely admit. No one talks about the *GoldenEye* engine, only how accomplished the game is. *Republic: The Revolution* and *Black & White* will succeed or fail on the quality of their gameplay, not the number of onscreen characters or polygon throughput.

Fundamentally, technology should be invisible: something developers seem to be forgetting. Few people notice how clever a game's underlying code is. Unless it's stupid.

But this current wave of technophilia seems symptomatic of the general turmoil in the industry. All hardware is undergoing a revolution. It's easier to argue what a certain technology can do rather than discuss how it could improve a player's experience. Who cares that Shiny's *Messiah* uses a realtime tessellation and deformation character engine? It's only important if it makes the body-shifting exploits of Bob the angel more believable.

The same is true of the endless cycle of triumphant announcements concerning the latest engine licensees: *Duke Nukem Forever* to use the *Unreal Tournament* engine; *American McGee's Alice Quake III*. But does anyone really think that *Daikatana* will be as good as *Half-Life* because they both rely on *Quake II* code?

With this in mind, it's been an instructive experience compiling **Edge**'s top 100 games. The only criterion was that games should be selected because of their continuing relevance, not because they were the first to demonstrate some new technological feature. Because great gameplay doesn't age like technology does.

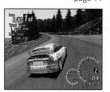

Many games boast impressive technical capabilities, including the likes of (from left to right) *Messiah*, *Daikatana*, and *Republic*. The crucial question, of course, is how well will the games actually play?

Edge's most wanted   Tips for the next millennium

Perfect Dark	Crazy Taxi	Team Fortress 2	Zelda Gaiden
(N64) Rare	(DC) Sega	(PC) Valve	(N64) Nintendo
With *Jet Force Gemini* and *Donkey Kong 64* out the door, Rare should be able to pull out all the stops for an Easter outing. But will Joanna Dark outshoot 007?	Variation within a genre is always something to be encouraged and true to its name *Crazy Taxi* is nothing if not innovative. Black cabs won't be the same.	Following its two big twitch firstperson shooters, the stage is set for *TF2*'s sophistication. Expect bigger levels and improved team structure.	It may be a case of more of the same, but when the quality of the original is so high this is one 'side story cash-in' that no gamer would refuse to buy.

PRESCREEN ALPHAS

HOT INCOMING PROSPECTS IN AN EXTENDED, END-OF-MILLENNIUM SPECIAL

GRAN TURISMO 2

FORMAT: **PLAYSTATION** DEVELOPER: **POLYPHONY DIGITAL, INC**

Gran Turismo 2 just missed out on making it into this month's reviews section. Unexpectedly, the game should now turbo its way into the Japanese market before January, although UK code is still not expected to hit European retailers until at least the end of January. At **Edge**'s most recent visit to SCEE's London HQ, it came to light that the technical data in the EU version has been written by *Top Gear* magazine journalists, another nod to authenticity. A further realistic touch is the in-game alloy shop, where a comprehensive selection of wheels from real manufacturers is available. Just watch all the Escort owners go for the three-spoke model…

BLACK & WHITE

With work on Lionhead's debut nearing completion, the various parts of the singleplayer game are coming together. So many new screens are being generated that they would not all fit in **Edge**'s cover feature this month (see p42). This selection shows the scale of the new environments. They include snow-capped mountains, verdant forests, and rolling valleys. Spells are also developing apace – **Edge** is particularly looking forward to exploring the variety which sees a whole village join together to create an enormous beast. As for the creatures, the tiger still gets **Edge**'s vote.

BERSERK

FORMAT: **DREAMCAST** DEVELOPER: **ASCII**

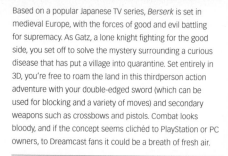

Based on a popular Japanese TV series, *Berserk* is set in medieval Europe, with the forces of good and evil battling for supremacy. As Gatz, a lone knight fighting for the good side, you set off to solve the mystery surrounding a curious disease that has put a village into quarantine. Set entirely in 3D, you're free to roam the land in this thirdperson action adventure with your double-edged sword (which can be used for blocking and a variety of moves) and secondary weapons such as crossbows and pistols. Combat looks bloody, and if the concept seems clichéd to PlayStation or PC owners, to Dreamcast fans it could be a breath of fresh air.

EVERGRACE

FORMAT: **PLAYSTATION2**   DEVELOPER: **FROM SOFTWARE**

Initially developed with PlayStation1 in mind, From Software has recently upped the stakes. A realtime 3D action RPG, *Evergrace*'s analogue control system resembles *Zelda*'s in intuitiveness. Enemies can be spotted from a safe distance and avoided if so wished. The game is divided between two dimensions, each featuring its own central character. As in *Ocarina of Time*, combat occurs in real time, but extra enemies attracted by the commotion may join the battle at any moment. Expect several types of magical spells plus weapon-assisted combat. A spring release is likely.

PARASITE EVE 2

FORMAT: **PLAYSTATION** DEVELOPER: **SQUARE**

SquareSoft's sequel to its first foray into the world of digital horror adventure was due out in Japan last month. Aya, the game's central character, returns in a more action-packed, *Resident Evil*-like approach. A new lock-on feature helps players target monsters, but as some of them have a limited perception range, it is possible to sneak past them, *Metal Gear Solid* style. The wide array of weaponry returns and Aya boasts several forms of parasite energy. Her repertoire and magical powers increase with fighting experience. *Evil 2* looks more than accomplished its predecessor; review next month.

THE BOUNCER

FORMAT: **PLAYSTATION2**   DEVELOPER: **SQUARESOF**

Recently confirmed as one of Square's PS2 launch titles (the company is currently working on at least a further eight titles for Sony's 128bit machine), *The Bouncer* continues to impress, with visual ambition and intriguing gameplay.

Characters appear to interact with nearly every object featured in the game (most can be picked up and used as weapons), though how the game links the fight sequences with some of the more action-packed cinematic aspects (such as running and jumping on to a departing train) remains to be seen.

If these sequences simply amount to cut-scenes, Square will have missed an obvious opportunity, although a tight timescale currently conspires against the company.

RIDGE RACER V

FORMAT: **PLAYSTATION2** DEVELOPER: **NAMCO**

The latest version of Namco's continuing racing saga is looking tasty. However, as one of PlayStation2's launch games, **Edge** would be surprised to find that *RRV* is little more than a significant visual leap over current PlayStation *RR* titles. There simply hasn't been enough time for PS2 developers to get to grips with the nuances of Sony's new hardware *and* be overly concerned with content.

But as an indication of the potential harnessed within the 128bit console, this appears to serve its purpose particularly well. Does anyone remember *Ridge Racer* on PS1 at all?

V-RALLY 2: MILLENNIUM EDITION

FORMAT: **DREAMCAST** DEVELOPER: **EDEN**

The Dreamcast version of Infogrames' rally franchise features 84 tracks, spanning 12 nations and involving 28 world rally cars. Like its PlayStation equivalent, a track generator and editor is promised, theoretically enabling an infinite number of stages and doing much to improve the game's lifespan.

Technically impressive fourplayer action, first seen on Sony's 32bit machine, will make an appearance, as should new handling, improved dynamics, and revised sound effects. The graphical quality to date is best described as satisfactory, and will provide an interesting point of comparison against PS2's first driving games.

GIANTS

FORMAT: **PC** DEVELOPER: **PLANET MOON**

Like many ambitious titles, Planet Moon's gorgeous shoot 'em up is suffering from the dreaded slippage. Still, with an Easter release now looking likely, it should provide the team with the necessary time to balance the three-way gameplay characteristics of Baz and his two Meccaryn sidekicks, Delphi the Sea Reaper, and Kabuto the eponymous giant.

New information from Planet Moon reveals that *Giants* will have both day and night settings. Some will be more interested in the possibility of a romantic link developing between Baz and Delphi – and the fact that her dress has been redesigned to make it shorter. (Sigh.)

BALDUR'S GATE II

FORMAT: **PC** DEVELOPER: **BIOWARE/BLACK ISLE**

Following the million-selling success of the Advanced Dungeons & Dragons-based original, *Baldur's Gate II* continues the storyline while introducing 15 new NPCs and 130 new spells into the game world. Twenty extra kits and classes have been introduced too, making it the most complete computer game based on AD&D.

Bioware's Infinity engine has also received a makeover, allowing it to support resolutions of up to 800x600, and 3D acceleration using the OpenGL API. The ability to play without the side menus open should ease the entry level, too.

Yellow?

COMING SOON...

gamecast™

email: info@gamecastuk.com for further details
gamecast is a trading name of fugue ventures ltd

SHOGUN: TOTAL WAR

FORMAT: **PC** DEVELOPER: **CREATIVE ASSEMBLY**

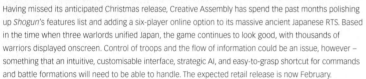

Having missed its anticipated Christmas release, Creative Assembly has spend the past months polishing up *Shogun*'s features list and adding a six-player online option to its massive ancient Japanese RTS. Based in the time when three warlords unified Japan, the game continues to look good, with thousands of warriors displayed onscreen. Control of troops and the flow of information could be an issue, however – something that an intuitive, customisable interface, strategic AI, and easy-to-grasp shortcut for commands and battle formations will need to be able to handle. The expected retail release is now February.

CRISIS ZONE

FORMAT: **COIN-OP** DEVELOPER: **NAMCO**

The third instalment of the *Crisis* series, *Zone* replaces the usual pistol peripheral with a machine gun – meaning the emphasis on accuracy is no longer as relevant. Presumably, a twoplayer version of the game is not offered as the challenge would be minimal. Most of the game remains faithful to its predecessor. A pedal mechanism still exists (though your character now carries a shield around with him so that hiding behind objects is no longer necessary), as does a time limit forcing you to either complete sections rapidly or reach into your pocket to dig out another £1 coin. A new twist, however, is the presence of a health bar on each of your adversaries. Three stages are offered, each with an obligatory boss character.

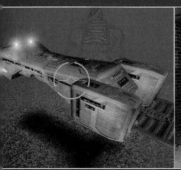

INVASION

This latest lightgun coin-op shooter is based on the amusing premise that an alien race helped humankind thousands of years ago, hoping the former would rapidly develop their intellectual capacity. Intent on gathering human brains to be used as ultimate CPUs to pilot the invaders' machinery, the aliens have returned to harvest their crop. It's up to you, either alone or in the company of a lightgun-toting friend, to stop them. Four stages based on US cities await clearing before a fifth stage (based inside the alien mothership) is accessible. Ground and airborne units feature throughout and your chrome-plated standard gun can be powered up to launch missiles or gain an autofire capability.

MEDIEVIL II

Continuing where its predecessor successfully left off (800,000 copies sold worldwide), *MediEvil II* sees Sir Dan Fortesque resurrected a second time (this time at the hands of evil magician Lord Palethorne) and travel through 17 open 3D levels needing thorough exploration if his task is to be successfully achieved. Set in a gothic version of Victorian London, the game has you visiting familiar locations such as Kew Gardens or Greenwich Docks, and the likeable features of the original title (puzzle-solving elements, vast range of weapons, plenty of well-designed enemies) have, of course, undergone further refinement.

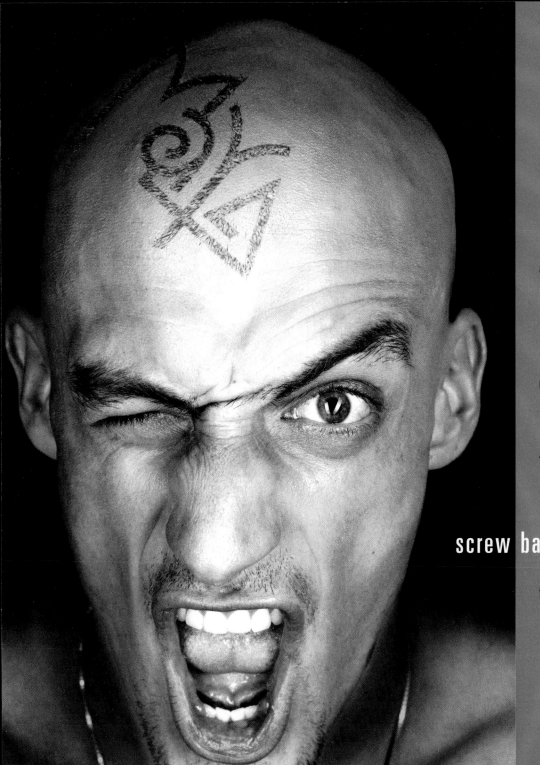

work hard, play hard.

according to **that** statement,

its all about **balance.**

why?

unbalanced people are

way more interesting.

true geniuses forget to put

their pants on in the morning.

screw balance!

find stuff that will make **work easier,**

so you can **play harder.**

MILLE MIGLIA

FORMAT: PLAYSTATION DEVELOPER: SCI

Based on the historic 1,000-mile race through Italy (a substantial portion of which consisted of perilous mountain roads responsible for numerous deaths), *Mille Miglia* features 18 classic cars (Ferraris, Alfa Romeos, Mercedes and Bugattis). An elaborate physics model and twoplayer mode are promised.

STRIDER 2

FORMAT: **PLAYSTATION** DEVELOPER: **CAPCOM**

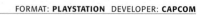

While the coin-op (developed on Namco's PS-friendly System 11 board) is scheduled to hit Japanese arcades on Christmas Day, the PS version should follow soon after on two CDs, one of them featuring the original 1989 arcade version. Both are expected to be identical to their respective sources.

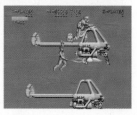

GUNLOK

Rebellion's squad-based action RPG is certainly based on an interesting premise. Sounding like *FFVII* crossed with *Millennium Soldier*, the game revolves around Gunlok, the first robot to dream, as he seeks to discover his origin and release his robot brothers from slavery. And helping him through the 15 different environments are four customisable characters. The PC-only title is looking for a publisher and is expected to be released in April

4 WHEEL THUNDER

Developed for Dreamcast by Bordeaux-based Kalisto, this monster truck/off-road buggy racer promises to run at a constant 60fps by the time it's released. Long outdoor tracks, featuring plenty of shortcut potential and indoor stadium-like courses are offered. Although only four cars race at a time, the developer is confident the resulting improvement in AI counterbalances the lack of on-screen opposition. At this stage the handling is promising.

THIEF 2: THE METAL AGE

FORMAT: **PC** DEVELOPER: **LOOKING GLASS**

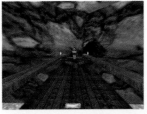

Despite the recent mission pack, Looking Glass is enhancing its sneaky FPS with a proper sequel. Using an enhanced version of the Dark Engine (as used in *System Shock 2*), the development team is making main character Garrett a better thief, not a better fighter. And true to the subtitle, plenty of weird gadgets, like camera grenades, should help out.

10SIX

Undergoing prolonged beta testing before it opens up to its potential one million online users, Segasoft's massive, persistent RTS PC game should appeal to the hordes who bought *Tiberian Sun*.

Based on a C&C-style planet, players can choose either a firstperson, thirdperson or a top-down view, as they mine Transium for cash and make alliances to protect their bases from those who would attack when they go offline.

RING

FORMAT: **DREAMCAST** DEVELOPER: **KADOKAWA**

Based on a novel (which was subsequently released in filmic form), *Ring* is another survival horror affair. Two worlds (real and virtual) divide the game, and you're able to travel between both, naturally. Many items can be used in both dimensions. Expect plenty of *Resident Evil/Tomb Raider*-type action.

GRAPHICS

DVD

SOUND

SPEAKERS

CD-RW

Digital music
Home cinema Internet
Games

Live the experience

Environmental Audio™

The Sims

What's a *Sim City* without its neighbours from hell? Edge twitches the net curtains and peers into Will Wright's latest wonder, a captivating dwelling simulator

Edge is having trouble with the neighbours. It's the music, you see. They just won't keep it down. It wouldn't be of such concern, but for the kids. Young Miyamoto and Carmack need their sleep, yet the Romeros next door won't stop partying.

Worse, it's in **Edge**'s own living room that they're partying. And the father of the house is joining in, jiving to what now seems an indulgent and unnecessary stereo. Zelda, the kids' mother, would tell the Romeros to get lost, but she's exhausted from cleaning up after the rowdy adults. She's at the point of collapse.

The domestic turbulence of Maxis' *The Sims* is more addictive than the average suburban soap opera, even though it didn't exactly spring from any great revolutionary zeal. Its inspiration was that most pedestrian of PC products, the two-a-penny 3D home planners that clog up magazine cover CDs and glossy ads for family PCs.

Creator **Will Wright** insists he's making games for fun. Well, with the *Sim City* series shifting over six million copies, he's certainly not doing it for the mortgage.

Click on a member of the household with your mouse pointer and a number of options appear. Here, the player has brought about interaction between two Sims

This is the third unhappy household to be created this afternoon alone. Even with a cheat mode racking up a line of credit that a Colombian drug baron wouldn't turn his nose up at, **Edge** is still coming up with 'The Simpsons' when attempting to create 'The Waltons'.

A lodger electrocuted himself mending the TV in the previous attempt, while an earlier mission to recreate the **Edge** office – complete with desks, PCs, sound systems and games consoles – ended badly when the corner hot tub became too tempting. Thinking about it, though, that's probably why there's no hot tub in the office.

"How's it going?" asks Wright, who ten years ago stole countless hours of your correspondent's life with *Sim City*.

"Ready for the interview?" asks Electronic Arts' press representative. "Ten more minutes," pleads **Edge**.

Nature or nurture?

"Whether they call it 'this house' or 'my house' is very telling," explains Wright, unclamping **Edge** from the PC.

"It reveals a lot about the empathy they feel for the households.

"If they've built up a house from scratch, they will refer to it as 'my house.' When they say 'their house' they're identifying more with the characters in the game."

But what does Wright want them to feel? Is this another *Sim City*-style experiment in social engineering, or a Tamagotchi-like opportunity for gamers to demonstrate their nurturing side?

"Actually, it goes back and forth a lot," he says. "In *The Sims* you control an entire family so there's no one character that's you. It removes that firstperson perspective – it's 'my family' but it's not 'me'. However, people will put their own family in and actually create their real-life house. Then they'll say 'my family and me'."

You're allowed to ponder these esoteric concerns when you have invented a genre and had it pretty much to yourself ever since. Having written the original Commodore 64 version of *Sim City* in 8,000 lines of machine code

The components you fill your household with depend on how much cash you have to spend. Countless items of furnishing are available

and founded his own publisher (because no existing outfit was prepared to take it on), Maxis, Wright has earned his lackadaisical approach.

With just a lone programmer, he's been exploring *The Sims* concept for more than two years. And despite it being just another product in Electronic Arts' enormous roster (the superpublisher acquired Maxis back in 1997) *The Sims* has garnered quite a reputation.

One view which emerges from colleagues is that *The Sims* is pure indulgence on Wright's behalf. The other,

Format: **PC**

Publisher: **Electronic Arts**

Developer: **Maxis**

Release: **January**

Origin: **US**

which **Edge** heartily endorses, goes something like "thank goodness somebody's trying something new."

A design for life

Wright doesn't see himself as a radical. A quiet, yet fiercely intelligent man approaching middle-age, he says he wouldn't have had to make *The Sims* if someone else had. For once you believe the cliché. "I was always fascinated by those architectural design programs," he insists. "They sell so many copies, but not many people are designing houses. I think that means people are using them as toys.

"Yet these programs are so finicky. They extract all the fun out of the process. We wondered what we'd have if we made it more fun and

A number of attributes, including tidiness, playfulness, etc, are set for each Sim at the start of the game. This chap (above left) is low on something obvious

less rigid – if we gave it the Lego-grid feel of *Sim City*."

The result is a piece of software that the BBC's 'Changing Rooms' team would lovingly take to their hearts.

Apart from the basic rules (your house must be a detached oasis set in suburbia, and the roof held up by the walls), anything goes.

You first design conventionally, laying down living rooms and kitchens as soon as you can, just to get your hands on the wonderful gadgets. By the time you tire of the boys' toys you start

to experiment with weirder architecture

Maxis staffers have built everything from army barracks complete with eight bunk dorms, to churches and, surely the epitome of an Englishman's castle, houses surrounded by moats where visitors must swim to the doorbell.

Television makeover programs are often criticised for creating inhospitable homes. Equally, in *The Sims*, placing the toilet next to the dishwasher or making an interior dividing wall out of fish tanks might make sense in the heat of the creative moment, but truly impractical

Maxis uses a stylised approach rather than attempting all-out realism in representing the Sims, as these FMV stills illustrate. The result is an almost cartoony world with a feel entirely of its own

To begin with, managing a household can be an absolute nightmare. An unattended stove can lead to minor disasters, and although the Sims will deal with problems on an autonomous basis, it's worth ushering their panicky forms along

designs would surely prove just that. How could Wright score one house against another? Only a human being could really tell whether the hall was just too long, or if the TV was simply too distracting if placed in the kitchen. The answer was clear – throw human beings into the mix.

Little Computer People

"By watching a simulated family living in the house we thought we could somehow use them to measure the efficiency of your architectural design," explains Wright.

Hence the eponymous Sims. The brand might be imported from *Sim City*, but these are Little Computer People as we've never seen them before. (Wright has only recently played the fondly remembered C64 game, although its producer, Rich Gold, now a researcher at Xerox Parc, is a personal friend.)

These pixel people argue, cook, feed the fish, and with time they inspire the sort of affection that even social miscreant Tamagotchi surely could only dream of. "The simulated people have become much more interesting than we'd hoped – and so the game has shifted more on to the people and less on to the house," Wright says.

The little patter of tiny feet brought Wright's houses to life, but he was cautious – doubtless chastened by the disastrously ambitious first take on *Sim City 3000*.

"Simulated people bring so many expectations in so many directions," Wright elaborates. "We had to make some hard choices. You will not see them go to work. They just leave the

The Sims have a 'stack' of priorities in their virtual minds. In this scene, for example, it's feasible that the Sim attending to the barbecue may feel the need to visit the bathroom, which in turn leaves a risk of burnt hot dogs

screen to go to work. You will not see them walking down the street. They'll go from one house to another discretely but you can't send them walking in the woods."

These decisions were partly driven by the desire to make a product rather than an impossible wish list. But they also came out of Wright's intimate understanding of a simulation player's mindset. "It's more to do with how the player plays the game than with the boundaries of the system," he explains.

"We could scroll the screen, and we

'These pixel people argue, cook, feed the fish, and with time they inspire the sort of affection that ever Tamagotchi surely only dreams of'

even had a prototype in which a little window showed Sims walking down the street, but our chosen approach helps compartmentalise the game in the player's head."

Other details are left to the gamer's imagination. A programmer's whim saw naked Sim body parts getting the Roger Cook fuzzy focus treatment. The team liked it so much it stayed in the game. And unlike Hollywood actors, these Sims exhibit the full range of human bodily functions. **E**

Sprawling abodes can be appreciated via a map-style overview (above). Players loaded with resources can build and maintain more than one residence at once

Excited? You should be.

MOVING THE
GAME ON

ATD

All the lights are on. But no one's home. Edge (eventually) catches up with Attention to Detail Ltd, a developer whose first project involved a blanket, a camera, a ghettoblaster and a never-ending supply of credits...

It's fair to say that **Edge**'s ATD visit starts weirder than most. Leaving the car in the designated area, **Edge** wanders into the barn-like building only to find the premises completely deserted. All the lights are on and the warm environment greets visitors wandering in from the cold. Assuming that some kind of refurbishment is underway, **Edge** negotiates two flights of stairs and arrives on the first floor only to be met by the same 'Twilight Zone' esque scenes as downstairs. No chairs, no tables, no funny little plastic figurines or anime posters littering the environment. Nothing more than a symmetric arrangement of neon tubes and wall-mounted radiators.

It transpires that this is indeed ATD's premises though only just converted and now awaiting the invasion of 70 employees and an army of computers, monitors, mouse pads and wires. For the moment, ATD still resides in a complex of buildings around the corner, only part of which belonged to the company when **Edge** last visited in 1995. These shiny new premises, as ATD's managing director **Chris Gibbs** explains, contrast with the company's humble beginnings.

"Activision wanted us to convert *Atari Super Sprint* from the arcade to the Atari ST," he recalls. The project was to occupy Gibbs and four university colleagues during eight weeks of their summer holidays at the end of their second year. However, while Activision was happy to send the quintet a "big truck full of Ataris and hard drives, some manuals and God knows what,'" the US publisher was unable to provide them with a *SuperSprint* coin-op until two weeks before the conversion was due.

"So we went down to our local arcade in Birmingham and we had a blanket, a ghettoblaster and a camera," Gibbs recalls. "We had a chat with the guy running the arcade who was very sympathetic and pumped the arcade full of credits. We put a blanket over our heads and sat there and played the game through every track and we photographed every screen and had a ghettoblaster recording the music."

For eight weeks every aspect of Atari's legendary coin-op was recreated with studious attention to detail and without any further support from Activision. "But we did it, we enjoyed it, we got it done on time," enthuses Gibbs. There was a glitch however. "We'd recorded all the music and put the tracks into the game but there was one left over. We scratched our heads and were up against deadlines.

"We thought there must have been some secret track we'd triggered when we played the game that we couldn't remember. Finally, one of the other students came back from holiday, heard the track and he said, 'That's from *Outrun*'. It was the arcade game right next to *SuperSprint* and we'd picked up that track while we were playing."

And that accounts for how it all began.

> ## We put a **blanket over our heads**, sat there and **played the game** through every track and **we photographed every screen** and had a ghettoblaster **recording the music**

Early **Edge** readers may remember ATD featured frequently during the magazine's early years, though it wasn't because of Gibbs and co's splendid ST *SuperSprint* conversion. As the company responsible for debugging the Jaguar hardware, ATD was one of the first developers to get its hands on Atari's '64bit' technology.

Base technology

"Very soon after we talked with **Edge** we were working on Jaguar CD – we did *BattleMorph* [sequel to ATD's early Jaguar title, *CyberMorph*] for Jaguar CD and *Blue Lightning* [a 64bit conversion of the Lynx game] – and it was totally apparent that that technology was being eclipsed," Gibbs states.

"I remember Sam Tramiel [then head of Atari] calling and saying, 'Hey, Chris, you know this *Battlemorph*, can you put loads of textures into it?' because they'd seen [*Total Eclipse*] on the 3DO and it was all beautifully textured, for its day, and there

MD Chris Gibbs (right) and technical director Fred Gill. Olympics project producer Nigel Collier looks at lead artist Pat Fox's work (far left)

Stage 2 offers more tracks, more vehicles and better visuals (PC version shown). There is much focus on the multiplayer aspects

we were with Gouraud-shaded polygons on the Jaguar. And Jaguar CD, well, it was just another storage medium, it wasn't changing the technology."

"The base technology didn't change at all and they were pushing it as a massive leap forward in the power of the Jaguar," **Fred Gill**, ATD's technical director and one of its founders, jumps in. "But Atari textured one of its own internal games, and it ran at about 5-6fps," he adds. "It wasn't bothered about gameplay, the game had to be fully textured just so that it could compete with all the other emerging technologies. It was a real shame," laments Gill, who's quick to praise his company's better handling of the situation. "We steered away from that battle, thank God, and it worked really well for us. We were able to keep frame rate up to 15-20fps which considering the amount of gameplay that was going on in *Battlemorph* was quite impressive."

Contractually compelled to complete its work with Jaguar CD, ATD missed the first wave of PlayStation and Saturn development but was then quick off the mark with *Blast Chamber*, an Activision-published action concept focusing on fourplayer action – then an apped area of the PlayStation market – released in October 1996. By its own admission, too much focus was spent on the multiplayer aspect to the cost of the oneplayer game.

The departure of two of the four founding members to pursue personal interests around this time allowed ATD to refocus solely on game development, renouncing the technological side of the proceedings (mainly video decompression techniques) that had formed part of the operation since its inception.

The bigger picture

In February 1997, ATD became part of the GBH group (Geoff Brown Holdings Ltd), which currently comprises fellow developer Silicon Dreams Studio (which ATD will soon face in a *Quake II* competition) and motion-capture specialist Audio Motion. ATD and Geoff Brown had dealt with each other previously – US Gold had distributed the ATD-developed *NightShift* and *Indiana Jones & Fate of Atlantis* for LucasFilm Games in the UK in the early 90's.

Joining GBH gave ATD an insight into Geoff Brown's vision of a developer which did more than just create games – one which looks after the PR elements, looks at licences, and marketing, which ATD had not considered until then.

The transformation was evident. *Rollcage*, a highly playable if occasionally frustrating futuristic racing title (7/10, **E**69), marked the developer's first release for GBH. At the time, the 15-strong team was bigger than any of ATD's previous projects

but it also marked the beginning of the company's application of a new model of development.

Gibbs explains: "The way we work is we have a five/six month period where you are trying to get the core technologies right. That's what you might call the prototype period. What we actually produce here is a concept document that's 30 or 40 pages long. It's not a sales document, it is a document that holds the vision of the game and rules out what it isn't. Then we do a number of things in parallel. We do a more detailed design document that tries to get to the nuts and bolts of the game, what specific gameplay elements are in there, what do things do…"

"Level descriptions, walk-throughs, power-ups, when they appear… absolutely everything that we can detail," adds Gill. "It's the production bible. If anybody's got a question, they can go to that document and everything that they want should be there. And it's a live document – some things you try don't work so you have to come back, revise them and work out the impact." A strict risk analysis policy dealing with technical and gameplay issues is applied during this prototype phase and if the team is not comfortable after the prototype period then the project is terminated.

One of ATD's current developments, a motorcycling title, has used this principle.

"The key issues for us were, 'Okay, let's look at all the competitors, why aren't motorbike games reviewing as highly as other racing games with four wheels? Where is the missing bit of fun? How do we solve that? Can we solve that?'," Gill reveals. "Within the prototype phase, initially four months, we solved a lot of problems. What we actually ended up with was another prototype phase – we raised some more issues. So that at the end of the prototype we have a method for generating all our in-game assets and also we know how long each of the phases takes and that can all be fed into the scheduling which happens at the end of the prototype. We've got very few risks in that product now. We're very comfortable with it in terms of our schedule estimates and what the gameplay is because we've already got it up and playing."

While ATD isn't allowed to disclose anything else concerning its motorcycling game, it is a lot more forthcoming about its next release, *Rollcage Stage 2*. Gibbs is quick to tackle the issue of sequels. "People buy sequels," he says. "And usually people buy more of a sequel than they do of the initial product . And they'll go on to buy a third one as well. The onus is on the developer to come up with more creative things they can do with the idea.

Sequels, sequels, sequels...

"Take *Rollcage*, because that's what we know. In the first one we had a car that could flip upside down and stick to walls and ceilings, and we could destroy scenery. It was essentially a racing game involving those elements. What we've done with *Stage 2* is produce more of a *Rollcage* 'party pack' – a big selection of games that you can play with that vehicle.

There's more racing than there was in the first one, but there are 15 other game modes for one and two players, so the motivation for playing it isn't just to win a race. I'm confident that what we've got in *Rollcage Stage 2* is a sequel that could never be criticised as, 'Oh, that's just the same thing with different track design'." And having had a taste of *Rollcage Stage 2*, **Edge** would have to agree with him.

In addition to the motorbike title, *Rollcage Stage 2* and a "PlayStation2 only [project] that concentrates very much on characters," ATD's other focus is on its Olympics-licensed products. Involving around 25 of its employees and to be released on "every format," this is possibly ATD's most ambitious venture to date. Collaborating with the Olympic Committee

Second time around for PS, the emphasis isn't solely on racing (and there is still plenty of that) but on the additional types of game offered

in Lausanne, Switzerland, the developer has been granted access to an unprecedented amount of information. In addition to an antipodean 'research' jaunt for some fortunate team members, all forms of official Sydney 2000 Olympics-related imagery have been made available, including official blueprints of all stadium buildings (which of course would pose a security threat if let out of the office, which explains project producer Nigel Collier's vigilance as **Edge**'s photographer wanders around the office). The amount of legal paperwork that has required signing is allegedly astounding.

Yet even with this amount of information, the title is an impressively accurate representation of the world's most-viewed sporting event. Everything from roof girders to the position of cameras is exactly as it is in real life and this authenticity extends to the way the characters are animated. It will be intriguing to see how the final product turns out when it's released next summer.

So this is where ATD is at the moment. "We are 70 people right now, we've three pretty full major teams and our plans are to have one more team. We won't go beyond that," admits Gibbs, "because the development doesn't require it for the projects we've got in mind for the next few years. We're part of a development group and the philosophy of that group is to have development studios and, if I speak with my GBH hat on, we would then look at starting up another studio rather than take either ourselves or Silicon Dreams and expand it further.

"So I'm very comfortable with the day to-day-running, the atmosphere of the

All Sydney 2000 Olympics imagery has been made available, including official blueprints of all staduim bulidings (a security threat if let out the office)

place. One more team would be a nice balance – for a good portfolio of products. We've got our Olympics stuff going on for the next few years and it would be silly of me to say that there are other genres that we're just going to stick to or we're going to avoid. Our games come from our people and we like to keep creativity at the forefront of what we're trying to do.

"There's no getting away from it, I think. If you like computer games, you like computer games. We've been doing it for 12 years and we played them before then, you know. And I don't think we'll ever stop doing that, really." E

Expect an unprecedented amount of detail when ATD's Olympics-licensed game turns up next year just before the real event begins

Black & Wh

IF THE DESIRE TO LOOK AFTER A PET IS PECULIARLY HUMAN, THE URGE TO CONTROL A 200-FOOT-HIGH TURTLE MUST BE STRANGELY GODLIKE – BUT THAT'S THE DRIVING FORCE BEHIND PETER MOLYNEUX'S GARGANTUAN MONSTER CLASH. WELCOME TO THE OVERSIZED WORLD OF BLACK & WHITE

Even the finished artwork displays the stark choices each player will have to face, to be good or evil

T he office sounds like a zoo and looks like a circus. Bellows and cries emanate from PCs and people are wandering around wearing animal masks. You expect Desmond Morris to peer through the blinds and start taking notes: 'The computer programmer is a strange beast, prone to flights of fantasy…'

Metaphorically at least, it's all in a day's work for the inmates at Lionhead. They may not normally wear masks to work, but to develop the most impressive game in the world they are hand-rearing animal avatars, teaching them the ways of life.

They are instructing their creatures about existence – eating, sleeping, defecating. Then they are adding the higher level actions that define man – love, religion and communication. At the centre of the melange, the inventor of the god game is about to don a pig mask and join in the fun.

More than most, **Peter Molyneux** understands the urge to nurture. When it came to pets, the other kids tangled with rabbits and kittens, but he's always had bigger plans.

"I once kidnapped a baby kangaroo from Windsor Safari Park," he confesses. "It was a long time ago, but my sister and I picked it up and bundled it into the back of the car." They got halfway home before a loud banging in the boot alerted their parents to the extra cargo.

It's exactly this feeling that drives *Black & White*. Wouldn't it be great to have a cool looking 200-foot-tall creature who will unconditionally love you?

Key to the game are the creatures'

abilities to mimic their god's behaviour. While you can teach a creature to do things, the surprise is it will learn independently by watching what you do. Just like a child, it will try to do the things its parent does.

And as suggested in the game's title, if you are a good god, your creature will also be good. Its physical appearance will morph, its colour taking on a holy golden hue. Conversely, evil deeds will turn a creature into a terrifying monster, complete with spikes and claws.

"The creatures reflect people's personalities," says Molyneux. Lionhead is now testing its creatures. Persistent minds push the limits of the AI code, while the artists work out the extremes of body morphing.

"Andy (Robson – head of testing) is a vicious bastard," Molyneux claims. "When he's on the football pitch he taunts people and sure enough his creature is a little bit vicious and can't be trusted. Jean-Claude (Cottier – 3D programmer) is the nicest person and his creature is lovely to deal with."

Black & White is more than a glorified, 3D Tamagotchi-style personality test, though. It takes the best bits from resource-management games, RPGs and god sims, and mashes them together. Molyneux is now calling the game the world's first god RPG.

He states: "*Black & White* is an RPG where you are a god: you play as a god and the choices that you have are of a god.

"It always aggrieved me in god games that there was this beautiful world but

there was always distance between you and the world – you weren't a physical presence," he continues.

"The creature is your physical representation in the world. He's the star of the show." Indeed, one of the striking aspects of the game is the bond that develops between players and their creatures.

"We did have a discussion about eating cows earlier today, didn't we?" coos Molyneux when he loads up his current favourite character, a tiger. The tiger picks up a cow, looks at it and then drops it, disinterested. The lesson that cows are for eating seems to have been forgotten.

"He's got a really nice purr," Molyneux demonstrates by stroking the tiger's belly with the onscreen hand icon. "He has also developed a little bit of a personality," he continues, the hand icon moving down the creature's abdomen.

"As he gets older he gets a little bit more sensitive about certain regions." The tiger's purr turns into a roar and he angrily tries to move out of the way. "You used to like it when you were a little baby," Molyneux gently chides.

A virtual paradise

For all its technology, the most common criticism levelled at *Black & White* is a perceived general lack of a specific plot.

"At the start you go through a very simple sequence where you get dragged into this land through the prayers of its people," says Molyneux.

"The land is called Eden, and before you arrive, it is a beautiful world, full of natural

Format: **PC/GBC**

Publisher: **Electronic Arts**

Developer: **Lionhead**

Release: **April**

Origin: **UK**

ite

Photography: Martin Thompson

The effects of evil will be obvious, as demonstrated by this fearsome wolf. In the finished game, the scenery will also morph to match playing styles

farm, which is a special creature that leaps up at your hand. You can click on this creature and transfer the mind of the creature you currently have into the mind of the turtle.

"So you have the baby turtle and a 100-foot ape. When you transfer the mind, the ape shrinks down and the turtle grows up. And you see all these cuts appear on the turtle – where all the scars were on the original ape."

These challenges, as they are called, drive the plot, pushing the player to make moral choices. "The little people in Eden pray to you," Molyneux says. "The way you react to these prayers dictates what you're like in the world."

The first challenge demonstrates this. A woman comes out of her house, falls to her knees and starts to pray. Her brother is lost in the forest and she is asking for your help to save him.

"What would you do?" Molyneux asks. Before **Edge** has a chance to answer, he has capriciously picked up the woman in his hand and tossed her into the sea to drown.

These challenges can give rewards, but there is no correct way to complete them.

taken from their own extremist viewpoints. It's likely that their visual form will become more esoteric in the final game.

The bigger picture

Players won't realise as they play, but *Black & White* is broken down into three different books. The first is simply about discovering the world, getting a creature and solving initial challenges. The second is triggered as the sea level drops, revealing more of Eden. It becomes apparent then that there are other gods and an overall god who wants to dominate the world.

"The third book is about the fight between your way of thinking and that of the other god," Molyneux reveals. "If you decide to be truly evil he will be truly good and vice versa."

And although that battle will conclude the single player game, there will be a lot more to *Black & White*. Most importantly, creatures can be saved and ported into multiplayer games, gaining experience as they go. There will even be a chat-enhanced version, called *Black & White: The Gathering* (see p48). And Lionhead has big plans for its wonder game.

"I can't talk about what we are planning after *Black & White*, but the persistent thing about the game is your creature," says Molyneux. "He is more persistent than any world that is created because he is truly, personally yours." One concrete plan is to support online aspects of the game and create a separate, five-person company called Black & White Ltd.

Beyond all issues of plot, gameplay and the challenges, the creature is *Black & White*'s killer app. The question is simple: wouldn't it be great to have a cool-looking 200-foot-tall creature who would unconditionally love you?

Or put it another way. Wouldn't it be great to steal a baby tiger or turtle from a zoo and take it home? And who knows, Lionhead might include a kangaroo, just for old time's sake.

beauty and wonder. The little people who live there lead an idyllic life without war and discord.

"It soon becomes clear that there are also some animals with powers that allow them to grow to enormous sizes. The first creatures you come across are three that walk out of the forest: a tiger, a cow

AS THE SEA LEVEL DROPS AND MORE OF EDEN IS REVEALED, IT BECOMES APPARENT THERE ARE OTHER GODS – INCLUDING AN OVERALL GOD WHO WANTS TO DOMINATE THE WHOLE WORLD

and an ape. They all leap up trying to grab your hand icon, and you get to chose one of them," says Molyneux.

These represent the three classes of animal in the game – aggressive, passive and neutral. Later you have the odd chance to change your creature.

"At one point you will discover a turtle farm," explains Molyneux. "Inside are two farmers with a problem. Their son has run off and they need him back. They pray to you and ask you for your help.

"Whatever way you chose to react, eventually you get one of the turtles in the

Playing as a good god and answering the woman's prayer may result in the village worshipping with more fervour and unlocking a new spell. Dropping some villagers off a mountain could similarly increase the amount of worship received by literally putting the fear of god in the remainder.

Moral aspects of the game are also highlighted via a struggle over your conscience. The place-holder graphics show a devil and an angel figure.

They fly around the screen offering advice on what course of action should be

■ COW

◼ Giles Jermy – spell programmer

■ GOAT

◼ Andy Robson – head of testing

■ LION

◼ Russell Shaw – head of music

■ BEAR

◼ Mark Healey – artist

■ TIGER

◼ Scawen Roberts – 3D programmer

TRIBES OF EDEN

The eight tribes are crucial to completing *Black & White*. While it's been said it will be possible to play without a creature, the tribes are the game's basic resource. Without their worship it is impossible to cast spells.

Organised into villages, each individual has a specific role and lifespan. Babies will be born and funerals held when important leaders die. But each village must be persuaded to believe in your godly power before access to their magic is granted. The more villagers that come to your citadel to worship, the more powerful you become as a god. But as spells are cast the worshippers become increasingly tired. They must be fed and given time off to enjoy themselves. One leisure activity that's available is football (right). Give them a football and watch an 11-a-side game, complete with spectators, commence.

Villages aren't completely loyal. Other gods can convert your followers and sap your power. And if you are not careful your creature could be worshipped too, with villagers taking him food, not bringing it to the citadel.

TIBETANS
THESE ARE THE MOST MYSTERIOUS TRIBE. ALL THAT IS KNOWN ABOUT THESE PEOPLE IS THEIR MAGIC, CONCENTRATED IN THE MYSTICAL REALM

AZTECS
WITH A HISTORY OF LIVE HUMAN SACRIFICES, IT'S NO SURPRISE THAT THE AZTECS' MAGIC REVOLVES AROUND EXTREMELY BLOODTHIRSTY AND VIOLENT SPELLS

The simplicity of *Black & White*'s interface is impressive. The onscreen hand icon is the only ingame tool. It is controlled by mouse movement. To move around the world, you simply pull the ground towards you. Any part of the world can be interacted with using the hand. Villagers, rocks and trees can all be picked up and carefully placed down or hurled high into the sky.

JAPANESE
THEIR SPECIAL POWERS HEIGHTEN THE MENTAL ASPECTS OF MAGIC – CONTROL OF JAPANESE TRIBES PROVIDES ACCESS TO ILLUSIONARY SPELLS

AMERICAN INDIANS
THE NATIVE AMERICANS ARE THE MOST PEACEABLE AND HELPFUL TRIBE ON EDEN. THEIR MAGIC DRAWS ON STRONG TRIBAL LINKS AND IS HIGHLY POSITIVE

A KIND OF MAGIC

The key to every god's power is the ability to use spells – defensively to heal and feed their people, and offensively to attack other creatures and tribes. Each of the 20 spells is represented by an icon, located on the citadel and activated using a gesture system. Clicking on the shield icon and then tracing a circle around the boundaries of a village will cause a blue forcefield to appear over it. A magic forest can be created wherever the mystic sycamore seed falls to the ground. This defensive spell slows attackers by forcing them to visit every tree in the forest before they can pass through. A more aggressive spell is the skeleton army (right). It's important to understand that spells can only be cast within the territory you control. They also take time to power up, giving opponents time to cast counter spells to protect themselves.

NORSE
THE VIKING TRIBES HAVE CONTROL OF FEARSOME MAGIC. THE TRUMP CARD IN THEIR ARSENAL IS THE TERRIFYING ABILITY TO SUMMON A SKELETON ARMY

GREEKS
EVERY GAME MUST HAVE ITS AVERAGE CHARACTERS. THAT ROLE IS PLAYED BY THE GREEKS. SADLY THEY POSSESS NO SPECIAL SKILLS OR MAGIC SPELLS

EGYPTIANS
TRUE TO HISTORICAL FORM, THE EGYPTIANS LOVE TO BUILD STRUCTURES. THEIR MAGIC ALLOWS YOU TO BUILD A DEFENSIVE WALL AROUND YOUR KINGDOM

CELTIC
THE GINGER-HAIRED CELTIC TRIBE PROVIDES POWER OVER EDEN'S WEATHER. THE CELTS' WORSHIP OPENS UP LIGHTNING AND STORM-BASED SPELLS

PERFECT BEAST

Just as Asimov had three rules of robotics, so Lionhead has three fundamental rules that control a creature's actions. They are:
1. I will not do anything that will cause me to die (incidentally the creatures are immortal)
2. I unconditionally love my god and everything I do, I will do to please him
3. I will try to achieve my god's ambition

Each creature must be taught the basics of life, such as eating and toilet training. They can even be named. But as they grow up they will learn to cast spells by watching their god's behaviour and that of other creatures as well. This is crucial as, unlike a god, a creature's power to cast spells is not limited by location, nor does it need people to worship it. If your creature sees you trying to attack another village it will lumber over and start casting spells as well.

There will be few things more awe inspiring in *Black & White* than a creature marching into one of your villages and casting the skeleton army spell.

Another key aspect of the creatures is their ability to morph. Starting in neutral shades and shapes, their physical appearance and AI will warp depending on the playing style of their god. And they will display different physical attributes such as fatness, thinness, strength and weakness, depending on how much exercise and food they receive.

There are 22 creatures in the game but only one type is playable at any time

RESTING PLACE

The citadel (below) is the hub of a god's power. It marks the centre of their territory. Built by villagers, it is the place they come to worship and chant. As the game progresses, its visual appearance mirrors the success of its god, becoming either larger and more powerful or progressively run down. On its battlements are displayed the icons for all the spells that are available.

The citadel functions as a guide to the history of *Black & White* as well. It's possible to go inside and check out a multitude of rooms. There's a creature room containing portraits of the creature at different stages, such as the first time he learned to eat. This room also contains a list of things he loves and hates. The challenge room displays the state of all the challenges that have been set up. Other rooms give access to the usual game options such as screen resolution and level of sound effects.

WORK OF A GOD

While *Black & White* offers a relatively freeform playing experience, Lionhead is aware that one criticism levelled is a lack of structure and plot. It will, however, be punctuated with 72 different challenges. These events will force players to consider how to react to specific events within their world. Not all of the 72 will be available. Different challenges will be triggered depending on the playing style and telegraphed using cut scenes (right).

One of the earliest examples concerns the prayers of two rich pig farmers. The village is low on food and they are using the situation to drive up prices. Some villagers have taken to sneaking into the farm and stealing livestock. The farmers pray for your help to stop this. It's not an obvious choice: either one decision condones the stealing as it punishes the farmers' greed while the alternative ignores the pain of the villagers. An alternative is to kill both the farmers and the thieves. These are the kind of moral dilemmas *Black & White* throws up.

BLACK & WHITE: THE GATHERING

MORE THAN JUST A GAME, PART OF THE **ONLINE ASPECT OF BLACK & WHITE**
LINKS INTO **TWO OF THE MOST POPULAR CHAT** PROGRAMS ON THE NET

Two months before the release of *Black & White*, Lionhead will take the brave step of releasing an online version. Known as *The Gathering*, it will be a free 10Mb download.

Launching with two servers, one in the UK and one at Origin in the US, it will allow users to go into a cut-down *Black & White* environment. Each landscape will support up to 32 users and will remain persistent as long as one person remains logged on.

Players will need to choose one of nine different creatures. Each has a preset AI personality. After its retail release, you will be able to upload your own personal creature into *The Gathering*. Crucially, you will also be able to save the creature's experiences and then take them back into the singleplayer game.

These worlds comprise several different zones, mirroring some aspects of *Black & White*. The fighting zone, for example, will contain rocks that can be thrown at rival creatures to practise combat, whereas in the competition zone you will be able to train your creature on running tracks. The play zone contains a village with chess, go boards and other activities. There will also be a magic zone containing different spells.

The aspect of *The Gathering* that Molyneux is most excited about is the way it will link in with popular chat programs – in particular AOL instant messaging and ICQ.

"*The Gathering* actually looks at your AOL and your ICQ friends list while you're playing," he says. "There's this little menu on the left-hand side of the screen which is the same as AOL and ICQ friends. It tells you whether they are online and whether they have *The Gathering*. If they do have it, you can send them a message. If they haven't got it you can email it to them."

Within the game, any text message typed into your computer will appear as a speech bubble coming from your creature.

Part chat, part *Black & White*, *The Gathering* has the potential to reach millions of users, taking text-based programs into a world of creature avatars and glorious 3D

"The incredibly cool thing is that if you and I are chatting away and another creature arrives but we really don't want anyone else to intrude, we can slap that creature away and continue our private chat," Molyneux explains.

Even more adventurous, the technology is in place for creatures to lip synch to words in realtime. This most recent development will not only support voice communication. "When I say 'hello', my creature will say 'hello,'" boasts Molyneux.

This raises some bandwidth issues, but as games such as Cryo's *Fireteam* are already supporting audio, it's obviously a technology whose time has come.

"Do you build a project with today's technology or do you build it for tomorrow's?" asks Molyneux rhetorically.

True to his passion for making *Black & White* a real mass-market game, he adds: "The only rule is don't make people with a slow machine and slow connections suffer. There are more sub P200s out there than there are post P200s."

AOL owns ICQ, and over 500m users worldwide have subcriptions to the company's chat facilities.

If *The Gathering* manages to attract just a tiny percentage of this userbase it will be a phenomenon giving Lionhead some serious server problems.

This is now the bottom line for *Black & White*. Bigger than *Quake III* just doesn't come close. Bigger than ICQ? Now you're talking.

Chat services like ICQ and AOL messaging will be integrated into *The Gathering*

gamecast™

coming soon... email: info@gamecastuk.com for details
gamecast is a trading name of fugue ventures ltd

The 100 best games of all time

It was never going to be easy, of course. But then it wasn't supposed to be *quite* such a demanding exercise, either. The idea was simple: gather the **Edge** team, plus a handpicked selection of gaming veterans with a close relationship to the magazine, and hammer out The List – a rundown of the 100 titles that best represent the pinnacle of computer and videogaming as a form of entertainment.

The criteria? Every game had to stand up to scrutiny in the harsh light of 1999. Were this merely a celebration of influential games, then there would be room for the likes of *Pong*, but in reality Nolan Bushnell's bat'n'ball legend is best left a fond memory from gaming's halcyon days.

Six hours, countless arguments, half a dozen pizzas, and one departure later, a tentative list of 100 titles had been drawn up. A further 56 games sat on a standby list, ready for the following evening, when the selectors reconvened. Interrupted only by some of most fiercely contested *International Track & Field* tournaments ever, the next eight hours saw a final rundown decided upon.

In much the same way **Edge**'s (eventual) nine judges found it extraordinarily difficult to pin down this hall of fame, there will be entries that you will disagree with. With this in mind, **Edge** will be opening a special Viewpoint slot in the coming months for the most convincing reader arguments. Which games do you think have been missed, and why? Does the number-one game really deserve its placing? Send your thoughts to the usual address.

However, before you go off and start writing in about the exclusion of *Super Mario Bros 3* or whatever, bear in mind that in cases such as this, only the standout title of the series (*Super Mario World*) has been included, for space considerations. Only if a further development in the series was significantly different in its approach (see *Super Mario 64*) was it deemed appropriate for inclusion.

Anyway, enough of that. On with the show…

STEVE JARRATT

EDGE'S LAUNCH EDITOR

MY ALL-TIME FAVOURITES...

Mercenary (C64) One of the first, true 3D action games. Even though it was just wireframe, it managed to generate a tremendous ambience and sense of mystery.
Elite (C64) Trading, shooting, docking – all simple stuff, but ridiculously entertaining.
X-Com (PS) Shamefully overlooked but incredibly playable strategy title.
Tetris (GB) How can your top ten not include this? Played it to death, still love it (especially in the challenge mode where the space shuttle takes off).
Street Fighter II (SNES) At the time this was simply the best one-on-one beat 'em up you could get – and the SNES version was far superior to the earlier Mega Drive version
Tomb Raider (PS) Forget the girl, forget the tits – praise the game's designers instead for this stunning and immensely captivating 3D platform adventure. One of the only games I've played for an entire Saturday, from breakfast till bedtime.
Ridge Racer (PS) What a top racing game. It looked gorgeous and played beautifully. Finally beating the Black Devil car was a huge relief…
Ocarina of Time (N64) What a fantastically atmospheric title. I loved playing this, still haven't finished it – which probably says more about me than the game. I will… when I get time.
Super Mario World (SNES) Probably the best 2D platformer of all time. Wonderfully inventive and challenging. Played to completion – and I'd still play it now.
GoldenEye (N64) Unsurpassed firstperson shooter. Tremendously challenging oneplayer mode, and still gets played in fourplayer, years after it arrived.
Plus **Super Mario 64** (N64), **Banjo-Kazooie** (N64), **Impossible Mission** (C64), **Defender of the Crown** (ST), **Mario Party** (N64), **Doom** (PC), and about 100 C64 games – I'm sad enough to still think it was the best games machine ever, for its time.

100 Super Punch Out!!

Format: **SNES**
Publisher: **Nintendo**
Developer: **In-house**
Date: **1994**

Edge issue: 01

Dreamcast *Ready 2 Rumble Boxing* recently proved how attractive the sport of pugilism can be in game form, but Nintendo was there years earlier with a title even more ridiculous in its conception, and more satisfying to play, too.

099 Solomon's Key

Format: **Coin-op**
Manufacturer: **Tecmo**
Developer: **In-house**
Date: **1986**

Edge issue: n/a

If publishers cannot manage to take the *Tetris* formula and tweak it to fashion a convincing puzzle game, what chance do developers have working from the ground up? Ask Tecmo: this enormously clever videogame is one of a kind.

098 Time Crisis

Format: **Coin-op**
Manufacturer: **Namco**
Developer: **In-house**
Date: **1996**

Edge issue: n/a

This is arguably the best ever lightgun game – chiefly due to the simple-yet-revolutionary addition of a 'duck' pedal allowing you to hide behind obstacles during firefights. A relentlessly exhilarating example of a much-maligned genre.

097 Choplifter

Format: **C64**
Publisher: **Brøderbund**
Developer: **Dan Jolin**
Date: **1982**

Edge issue: n/a

Taking its cue from *Defender*, *Choplifter* took a fantastical wartime scenario and threw it into a fast-paced airborne shoot 'em up environment where rescuing hostages became a ridiculously compelling pursuit. Simplistic but groundbreaking.

096 Phantasy Star III: Generations of Doom

Format: **MD**
Publisher: **Sega**
Developer: **In-house**
Date: **1991**

Edge issue: n/a

This epic and engrossing adventure kept Mega Drive owners shut off from the outside world for long periods of time as they battled their way through three generations of characters in an experience that rivals some of Square's finest.

095 Syndicate

Format: **Amiga**
Publisher: **Electronic Arts**
Developer: **Bullfrog**
Date: **1993**

Edge issue: n/a

This cyberpunk action strategy title takes concepts from the usual sources (*Blade Runner*, *Neuromancer* et al) and builds them into a compelling game of corporate subterfuge, violence and strategy. The action – which has you controlling a megacorp attempting to exert bloody control over a futuristic city – is involving and addictive.

094 NBA Jam

Format: **SNES**
Publisher: **Acclaim**
Developer: **Iguana**
Date: **1994**

Edge issue: n/a

Iguana's SNES version of *NBA Jam* is still one of the most addictive multiplayer experiences available. Matches between four skilled individuals often reach proportions rarely attained by even the freshest multiplayer titles.

Strider

093

Format: **Coin-op**
Manufacturer: **Capcom**
Developer: **In-house**
Date: **1989**

Edge issue: n/a

They certainly don't make them like this any more. Why? Because the levels of action evident in a game such as this simply cannot be conveyed within a 3D environment. *Strider* is a showcase for fast-paced, pyrotechnics-drenched action, ramming set-piece after set-piece down the gamer's throat. A benchmark in 2D arcade gaming.

Wipeout

092

Format: **PS**
Publisher: **Psygnosis**
Developer: **In-house**
Date: **1995**

Edge issue: 25

A fusion of supreme audio and visual content, *Wipeout* heralded a new, distinctive era in game production. Psygnosis' Liverpool studio at its best, this initially unfriendly racer succeeds in delivering convincing gravity-defying action.

Boulderdash 2

091

Format: **C64**
Publisher: **First Star Software, Inc**
Developer: **In-house**
Date: **1985**

Edge issue: n/a

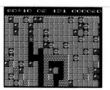

The wonderful thing about *Boulderdash* (which has you running around a subterranean arena searching for diamonds) is the open, complex gameplay, with hundreds of ways to complete each stage, none of them obvious. Timeless.

Paradroid

090

Format: **C64**
Publisher: **Hewson Consultants**
Developer: **Andrew Braybrook**
Date: **1986**

Edge issue: n/a

The high point in Andrew Braybrook's coding career, *Paradroid* mined a rich seam of SF influences to deliver an experience unlike any that had preceded it. If ever a game deserved bringing bang up to date, surely this is it.

Asteroids

089

Format: **Coin-op**
Manufacturer: **Atari**
Developer: **In-house**
Date: **1979**

Edge issue: n/a

It doesn't get much more primal than this. And that's the reason why *Asteroids* still stands up today: with such a limited number of factors coming into play, but each balanced so perfectly against another, classic twitch gaming is assured.

Lemmings

088

Format: **Amiga**
Publisher: **Psygnosis**
Developer: **DMA Design**
Date: **1991**

Edge issue: n/a

An innovative and addictive puzzler that encourages leftfield thinking. Who'd have thought that guiding small mammals from one side of a level to another could ever be content for classic gaming? Yet that's just what this is.

Nemesis

087

Format: **Coin-op**
Manufacturer: **Konami**
Developer: **In-house**
Date: **1985**

Edge issue: n/a

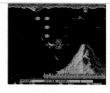

The first in the series (aka *Gradius*) remains the most finely tuned of the lot. Konami set out a number of templates with this title, which stands as one of the most convincing updates of a proven standard – in this case *Scramble*.

MARTIN HOLLIS

DIRECTOR, GOLDENEYE

MY ALL-TIME FAVOURITES...

Exile (BBC) The 2D sci-fi side-on platform-style graphic adventure carried to the absolute extreme. Particle systems, flocking, speech, and real puzzles for nuclear physicists.
NetHack (Unix) Unfettered by sound and graphics the gameplay triumphs in this odyssey through automatically generated dungeon mazes and the entire menagerie of Brewer's Phrase and Fable as played by all typographical symbols. 'You cannot pick up the +2 cursed wand of polymorph because you are levitating. Your cat dies.'
Repton 2 (BBC) This 2D push-and-collect-'em-up was so sprawling and puzzle heavy it hurt my head for years. Despite my mapping software and other reverse engineering I have still not collected all 4,744 diamonds. The 16 bars of Scott Joplin argue persuasively against music in videogames.
Minefield (PC) A tense combination of logic and luck. Best played with a time limit.
The Sentinel (C64) The grinding sound was spine chilling and being absorbed by an alien is definitely one of my least favourite things.
Sokoban (Mac) 'Less is more' applied to the pushing puzzle game. Many levels are obviously impossible – right up until the moment you solve them.
Super Bomberman (SNES) The multiplayer game ate my lunchbreaks and then broke my hand. So addictive it should be illegal.
Lemmings (Amiga) The small sprites overloaded my few cuteness receptors – never have so many cared so much about so few pixels. The gameplay itself was incredible mostly because of the capability for environment modification. The haunting music stays with you forever. ('How much is that doggy in the window?')
Elite (BBC) A world changer with astronomical scope, many graphical innovations, and intelligent compromises between reality and entertainment. A unique blend of murder in the far distance, shopping, and wandering the galaxy trying to pronounce the exotic (unpronounceable) place names. Computers good. Narcotics bad. Fugitive status. Thargoid ambush. Military lasers. Alien items. Right on, commander!!!
Zelda III: A Link to the Past (SNES) I am not worthy.

086 Xenogears

Format: **PS**
Publisher: **Square Electronic Arts**
Developer: **In-house**
Date: **1998**

Edge issue: **67**

Basic in presentation terms compared to the mighty *Final Fantasy* series in its PlayStation guise, *Xenogears'* more classical approach remains wholly convincing. And when it does innovate – with mecha combat – it really shines.

---

085 Legend of the Mystical Ninja

Format: **SNES**
Publisher: **Konami**
Developer: **In-house**
Date: **1991**

Edge issue: n/a

Despite numerous sequels – in 2D and 3D – Konami never quite recaptured the magic that marked this out as a landmark in 16bit videogaming. Released at a time when mainstream gamers had little idea of just how inventive Japanese designers could be, *Mystical Ninja* oozed wit and flair. A truly memorable gaming experience.

DAVID DOAK

PROGRAMMER/DESIGNER,
FREE RADICAL DESIGN

MY ALL-TIME FAVOURITES...

Bomberman (SNES) Probably the best multiplayer game ever. What more can I say?
Super Mario Kart (SNES) Somehow the cheating saccharin characters don't matter.
Zelda III: A Link to the Past (SNES) Unfolds beautifully. Precisely crafted levels set in an inspired mirror world which remains a joy to explore right through to the end.
Zelda IV: Link's Awakening (Game Boy) Helps to make the thumb-cramping hours squinting at that tiny screen just fly by.
Xpilot (any box with X Windows) A triumph of gameplay over graphics – massively multiplayer, Internet-server based, and configurable long before everyone else jumped on the bandwagon. Go on, delete your Windoze, install Linux and give it a try.
Monkey Island I & II (PC) Quirky humour seldom misses and still the pinnacle of point-and-click adventuring.
Defender (coin-op) The discerning addict's choice for a superior 60-second fix – which is about how long I last.
Missile Command (coin-op) What trackballs were invented for – plus adrenochrome graphics and a choice of LED-equipped firing buttons but just never quite enough time to decide exactly which one to fire from.
Space Duel (coin-op) A take on the *Asteroids* theme with the added insane genius of linking two players together to create the videogame equivalent of a three-legged pub crawl.
Peter Pack Rat (coin-op) A platformer with loads of embellishments. It was all we had down our college bar for ages.
Laser Squad (Spectrum) Turn-based perfection in 48K. The asymmetry of 'Assassins' scenario with two players is still a masterpiece.

---

084 Thrust

Format: **C64**
Publisher: **Firebird**
Developer: **Jeremy Smith**
Date: **1985**

Edge issue: n/a

When the concept of cheap software was still in its infancy, one title more than any other proved that £2.50 could still but an awful lot of game. Inspired by *Gravitar*, *Thrust*'s classically tricky gameplay truly separates the men from the boys.

---

083 Super Pang

Format: **Coin-op/various**
Publisher: **Mitchell Corp**
Developer: **In-house**
Date: **1990**

Edge issue: n/a

If some of the titles here prove how complexity can benefit gameplay, the likes of *Super Pang* show how the most basic (and, truth be told, daft) of premises can result action to die for. Another triumph for single-plane gaming.

---

082 Populous 2

Format: **Amiga**
Publisher: **Electronic Arts**
Developer: **Bullfrog**
Date: **1991**

Edge issue: n/a

Two tribes share a single landscape, the player acts as one tribe's god and aims to dominate the planet. The control system, which has you manipulating the environment is revolutionary. The near chess-like gameplay still entices today.

---

081 Marble Madness

Format: **Coin-op**
Manufacturer: **Atari**
Developer: **In-house**
Date: **1984**

Edge issue: n/a

A beautiful game not in only in concept (control a marble over surreal obstacle courses via trackball? Genius), but in audio and visual terms, too. A true coin-op legend: rarely again would one machine stand so far apart from its peers.

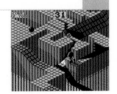

---

080 NHL '98

Format: **PS**
Publisher: **EA**
Developer: **In-house**
Date: **1997**

Edge issue: n/a

While the latest version offers an overly cluttered representation of the world of ice hockey, EA perfected its series back in 1997 with superb presentation supported by great visuals, excellent sound effects and, crucially, tight gameplay.

Gauntlet II 079

Format: **Coin-op**
Manufacturer: **Atari**
Developer: **In-house**
Date: **1986**

Edge issue: n/a

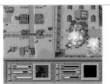

As today's game designers have discovered, multiplayer is where the hottest action is at, the addition of human-versus-human interaction bringing a magic factor 'X' into the experience. Atari knew this in the mid-'80s: this is the proof.

Chu-Chu Rocket 078

Format: **DC**
Publisher: **Sega**
Developer: **In-house (Sonic Team)**
Date: **1999**

Edge issue: 80

A stupefyingly simple concept supported by cute visuals ends up delivering one of the most addictive console multiplayer experiences around. Hardly surprising considering the gameplay-driven Sonic Team is behind the project. No Dreamcast owner with more than two friends should miss out on this utterly fabulous experience.

Return Fire 077

Format: **3DO**
Publisher: **Studio 3DO**
Developer: **Baron RK Von Wolfshield**
Date: **1994**

Edge issue: 19

If there's one thing Trip Hawkins' format could do, it was take existing concepts and make them look a whole lot more welcoming. Thus, Microillusions' *Firepower* became the supreme game of warfare it always promised to be.

Bomb Jack 076

Format: **Coin-op**
Manufacturer: **Tehkan**
Developer: **In-house**
Date: **1984**

Edge issue: n/a

In some respects a natural successor to *Pac-Man*, *Bomb Jack* is the quintessential game of high scores. With tight play areas and scarily devious enemies, this is the kind of experience to remind designers how to engineer 'drive'.

Galaga 075

Format: **Coin-op**
Publisher: **Namco**
Developer: **In-house**
Date: **1981**

Edge issue: n/a

The static-screen vertical shooter came of age when Namco used this to update its seminal series of space combat that started with *Galaxian*. Retaining a simplicity necessitated by hardware, *Galaga* offers up a venerable challenge that stands the test of time like few others.

Pac-Man 074

Format: **Coin-op**
Publisher: **Namco**
Developer: **In-house**
Date: **1980**

Edge issue: n/a

A game that, 20 years since appearing, still delivers levels of enjoyment surprisingly close to those of its heyday must be something special. A stupidly simple concept, Namco's 1980 arcade title may not quite offer *Tetris*-like levels of addictivity, but it certainly stands on its own two feet.

Rampart 073

Format: **Coin-op**
Manufacturer: **Atari**
Developer: **in-house**
Date: **1990**

Edge issue: n/a

On paper, the idea – take *Tetris* and meld it with castle-assaulting combat, over turns – absolutely reeks. And in the hands of a lesser developer the title may have stank, but an in-form Atari brought multiplayer gaming to new heights.

FREDERIC RAYNAL

CREATIVE DIRECTOR, NO CLICHÉ

MY ALL-TIME FAVOURITES…

Manic Miner (Spectrum) This is the first game that really amazed me. For me, it was the real beginning of platform games.
Alien 8 (Spectrum) First puzzle game in 3D. I fell in love with isometric 3D through this one.
Marble Madness (coin-op) I literally wore out my fingers with its trackball.
Nibbler (coin-op) I did a version of this caterpillar game on every computer I owned.
Zelda III: A Link to the Past (SNES) Action/adventure is my preferred type of game and I learned so much from this one.
Alone in the Dark (PC) Sorry, but it was the first big commercial game I created, where I was completely free. I put everything I'd been loving in other games into it.
Carmaggedon 2 (PC) I love car racing games. The gameplay was so different from other car games. Disregarding the gore aspect, the gameplay and the construction were solid.
Little Big Adventure 2: Twinsen's Odyssey (PC) Sorry again. I love 3D action/adventure games. As I make games I want to play, this one is really my favourite.
Legend of Zelda: Ocarina of Time (N64) Action/adventure again. No comment.
Age of Empires (PC) The only strategy game I like. I wish that all games were as well done than this one.

HIDEO KOJIMA

DIRECTOR, METAL GEAR SOLID

MY ALL-TIME FAVOURITES...

Super Mario Bros (Famicom) The game that showed me for the first time the simple but deep enjoyment of games (action games in particular). I wouldn't have joined the videogame industry if I hadn't seen this.
Xevious (coin-op) Till then backgrounds were always black or the universe. In this game, however, there was green vegetation and a detailed world created. This taught me that it was possible to create a world in the game medium. I bought the Famicom console to play this game at home.
Portopia Murder Case (Famicom) This Enix game taught me that one can tell a story and develop plots around a scenario in the game genre – a very impacting moment very different from then-conventional action games.
Outer World (Super Famicom) An independent film-esque game with outstanding world details, effects, gameplay. Very strong influence of the 'writer'.
Operation Wolf (coin-op) My favourite gun shooting game that got me really excited. (I personally thought Operation Thunderbolt was more exhilarating.)
Legend of Zelda III: A Link to the Past (Super Famicom) My favourite game by Mr Miyamoto

072 Contra III

Format: **SNES**
Publisher: **Konami**
Developer: **In-house**
Date: **1992**

Edge issue: n/a

Balls-out action gaming at its most gratifyingly base. Konami has tried time and again to resurrect the spark evident in this masterful twoplayer scrolling shooter, but this Japanese-produced *Gryzor* update remains the daddy.

071 Shinobi

Format: **Coin-op**
Manufacturer: **Sega**
Developer: **In-house**
Date: **1987**

Edge issue: n/a

With some of the most considered gameplay you'll ever see in an action title, *Shinobi* sits uncomfortably alongside other Sega titles of its era such as *Space Harrier*. Without doubt, the king among 2D scrolling actioners of the '80s.

070 Grand Theft Auto

Format: **PC**
Publisher: **Gremlin**
Developer: **DMA Design**
Date: **1997**

Edge issue: 52

Bucking the trend for 3D environments, *GTA* excels in finely tuned gameplay and offers a cartoon-like top-down view of a crime-rife city. DMA's immensely entertaining game hooks all those prepared to venture into its world.

069 Exile

Format: **Amiga**
Publisher: **Audiogenic**
Developer: **J Smith/P Irving**
Date: **1991**

Edge issue: n/a

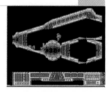

Part *Lunar Jetman*, part science lesson, *Exile* remains an untouchable title, if only because its component parts hang together so convincingly. An adventure driven by action, this is one of the most absorbing experiences ever realised.

068 The Sentinel

Format: **C64**
Publisher: **Firebird**
Developer: **Geoff Crammond**
Date: **1986**

Edge issue: n/a

A minimalist, almost sinister-feeling experience, *The Sentinel*'s reputation as a milestone in cerebral gaming is well deserved. Mild chess influences play out over an insane amount of hypnotic levels to create a legendary challenge.

67 Mercenary

Format: **C64**
Publisher: **Novagen**
Developer: **Paul Woakes**
Date: **1986**

Edge issue: n/a

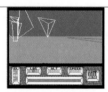 

The feeling of tumbling into a living, breathing alternate universe has rarely been evoked as convincingly as in *Mercenary*, even despite the game's naturally limited wireframe-3D environments. Dark humour – running at odds with the technology on display – is just one layer of this most rich of 8bit space adventure experiences.

066 Super Sprint

Format: **Coin-op**
Manufacturer: **Atari**
Developer: **In-house**
Date: **1989**

Edge issue: n/a

Furious threeplayer action in a title that even when released offered little visual impact to speak of. Yet what it lacks in aesthetics (or car dynamics, for that matter) it more than makes up in playability. As a package, it has few peers.

Head Over Heels
065

Format: **Spectrum**
Publisher: **Ocean**
Developer: **J Ritman/B Drummond**
Date: **1987**

Edge issue: n/a

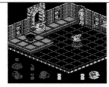

Patently inspired by Ultimate's *Knight Lore* and *Alien 8*, *Head Over Heels* manages to surpass both by delivering a world in which the eponymous characters must conspire in order to succeed. Level design is rarely anything short of delightful, while the graphics bear detail whose bitmapped charm outstrips any number of polygons.

Defender
064

Format: **Coin-op**
Manufacturer: **Williams**
Developer: **Eugene Jarvis**
Date: **1980**

Edge issue: n/a

A celebration of stark, neon sprites driven at warp speeds, *Defender* still rocks the bells today. The game's unconventional control setup serves only to cement its reputation as the quintessential old-school arcade-goer's title.

Elite
063

Format: **BBC model B**
Publisher: **Acornsoft**
Developer: **In house**
Date: **1984**

Edge issue: n/a

Elite still offers something unique: totally open gameplay. You get a spaceship, a few hundred credits, and a galaxy – what you do with them is your business. *Elite* flatters rather than replaces the participant's imagination. A true one-off.

The Need For Speed
062

Format: **3DO**
Publisher: **EA**
Developer: **In-house (EA Canada)**
Date: **1994**

Edge issue: 16

3DO's version of EA's franchise was not only the first but easily the best, and it still outshines many of today's driving titles. Why no one has properly updated the concept (realistic road racing among civilian traffic) is remarkable.

Virtual Fighter 2
061

Format: **Coin-op**
Manufacturer: **Sega**
Developer: **In-house (AM2)**
Date: **1995**

Edge issue: 28

Taking advantage of Model 2's rendering performance, *VF2* added ultra-smooth fighter movement and subtle texture maps to an already formidable gaming concept. This is the beat 'em up genre at its most hardcore.

Sonic the Hedgehog
060

Format: **MD**
Publisher: **Sega**
Developer: **In-house**
Date: **1990**

Edge issue: n/a

The sequel's levels may benefit from better design, but the Sega mascot's original platforming adventure delivers the best gameplay. Inspiring environments, hidden rooms and more: Sonic gracefully span his way into videogaming history.

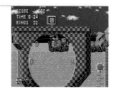

Sensible Soccer
059

Format: **Amiga**
Publisher: **Renegade**
Developer: **Sensible Software**
Date: **1992**

Edge issue: n/a

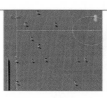
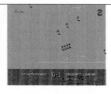

Having completed *Microprose Soccer*, Sensible looked at what Anco was doing with *Kick Off*, then fused the two, drew back the game camera, threw in a selection of carefully considered extras, and came up with an instant classic. After all this time, *still* regarded by some to be the ultimate representation of the beautiful game.

TOBY GARD

CREATIVE DIRECTOR,
CONFOUNDING FACTOR

MY ALL-TIME FAVOURITES...

Ultima Underworld (PC) Excellent level design, nice story and great character advancement in a 3D engine that was years ahead of it time.

EverQuest (PC) The first online game to really wipe out a significant part of my social life.

Super Mario 64 (N64) You have to get all 120 stars. The game is so good it leaves you no other option.

Legend of Zelda: Ocarina of Time (N64) There are simply too many good bits to even start describing.

Full Throttle (PC) Ben is probably *the* coolest game character ever made, and funny to boot.

X-Wing (PC) The template for all the other space battle games of note ever since.

Power Stone (Dreamcast) The first 3D fighting game that actually plays in 3D instead of just using a 3D engine.

Stunt Island (PC) An old PC game where you set up your own stunts and then filmed and edited them together – endless fun for people who want to be directors.

Spindizzy (Spectrum) Great physics-based gameplay with really imaginative, cunning level design – on the Spectrum.

Bomber Man (SNES) There is nothing better than to chill out with friends playing a bit of *Bomber Man*.

**CHRIS KINGSLEY &
JASON KINGSLEY**

CTO & CEO, REBELLION

MY ALL-TIME FAVOURITES...

1. Space Invaders (coin-op) We still remember playing it the first time, seeing the invaders get faster and faster as you shot more of them. And it was in colour, too. Well, coloured gel over a monochrome screen!
2. Paradroid (C64) This had all the classic ingredients. Just a brilliant game.
3. Adventure (Atari VCS) This had three dragons (red, yellow and green). You could carry a sword and a chalice (but not at the same time) – the chalice really looked gold because of the cool colour cycling. Still got it and play it occasionally on our Atari VCS.
4. Star Raiders (Atari 800) Has to be one of our all-time favourites. We remember reading about this and the amazing new Atari 800 home computer in a Maplin catalogue. We still have a working copy on our still working Atari 800, and we still play it. Most amazingly of all, they got the whole game into 8K!
5. Wizard of Wor (Atari 800) This was an excellent maze arcade game. We got the Atari 800 version as soon as it came out. It was one of the first twoplayer games, and it really showed the potential for multiplayer gaming.
6. Defender (coin-op) Probably one of the most difficult arcade games to master because of the number of controls, but it had great graphics and a lot happening on the screen.
7. Sinistar (coin-op) Has to be on the favourites list. A fiendishly difficult arcade game, but one of the first games with speech in it. It was total panic when you heard 'I hunger' and 'I am Sinistar'.
8. Xevious (coin-op) This was a very cool arcade game, with great graphics. It was just great fun to play.
9. Scramble (coin-op) This inspired us both. Chris even wrote a version of this on his Commodore PET.
10. Early text-based adventure games like **The Pawn** and Scott Adams' titles.

---

058 Daytona USA

Format: **Coin-op**
Manufacturer: **Sega**
Developer: **In-house (AM2)**
Date: **1994**

Edge issue: **07**

Forget the limp Saturn conversion – coin-op *Daytona* is the only way to travel. With eight cabinets linked (and, crucially, seven friends available to play against), the Sega driving experience reaches levels of near nirvana.

---

057 Death Tanks

Format: **Saturn**
Publisher: **BMG Interactive**
Developer: **Zombie**
Date: **1997**

Edge issue: **n/a**

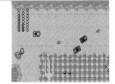

As a bonus game shipped as part of Egyptian-themed firstperson shooter *Exhumed*, *Death Tanks* is extreme multiplayer console gaming *par excellence*. Horrendously limited visuals hide unfussy design that is simply to be marvelled at.

---

056 Micro Machines 2

Format: **MD**
Publisher: **Codemasters**
Developer: **In-house**
Date: **1994**

Edge issue: **15**

If games were measured by simplicity above all else, the *Micro Machines* series would surely be the most critically acclaimed of all time. Largely irrelevant in oneplayer mode, with three friends instalment number two is manna from heaven.

---

055 Speedball 2

Format: **Amiga**
Publisher: **Renegade**
Developer: **The Bitmap Bros**
Date: **1988**

Edge issue: **n/a**

Truly a product of its time, making use of the graphical capabilities of the day's 16bit micros and a spirit of innovation yet to be tainted by commercial pressures, *Speedball 2* is that rarest of breeds – a future-sports game that works.

---

054 Stunt Car Racer

Format: **Amiga**
Publisher: **Firebird**
Developer: **Geoff Crammond**
Date: **1988**

Edge issue: **n/a**

Ahead of the realism of *F1 GP*, veteran coder Geoff Crammond made this demanding futuristic racer based on series of twisting, turning, looping circuits all narrower than a supermodel's waist. Challenging and compulsive.

---

053 OutRun

Format: **Coin-op (deluxe)**
Manufacturer: **Sega**
Developer: **In-house (AM2)**
Date: **1986**

Edge issue: **n/a**

The ultimate coin-op experience? Perhaps. It's certainly true that, in its deluxe incarnation, *OutRun* changed gamers' perceptions of the potential of arcade gaming to a larger degree than anything since, such were the overwhelming levels of audio-visual it threw at you. Finding such a beast is difficult nowadays, but well worth the effort.

---

052 Bubble Bobble

Format: **Coin-op**
Manufacturer: **Taito**
Developer: **In-house**
Date: **1986**

Edge issue: **n/a**

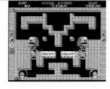

An action game that managed to garner a huge female following? Yes. While girls were waiting for their boyfriends to finish playing *Street Fighter II* they were indulging in this, one of the most compulsive platform games ever created.

Sonic Adventure
051

Format: **DC**
Publisher: **Sega**
Developer: **In-house (Sonic Team)**
Date: **1998**

Edge issue: 68

Sonic's first 'proper' venture into 3D is a success. It may have lost some of the original Mega Drive series' character, but *Adventure* proudly displays the hallmarks of Sonic Team, with frequently masterful touches of imagination and graphical flair that does justice to Sega's 128bit technology. Rough edges aside, a dreamy title.

R-Type
050

Format: **Coin-op**
Manufacturer: **Irem**
Developer: **In-house**
Date: **1988**

Edge issue: n/a

Never bettered – by its own successors or those that sought to steal Irem's crown – *R-Type* is a relic from the '80s worth preserving. Its powerup system has never been bettered in terms of ingenuity. Scrolling shooters don't get any better.

Robotron 2084
049

Format: **Coin-op**
Manufacturer: **Williams**
Developer: **Eugene Jarvis**
Date: **1982**

Edge issue: n/a

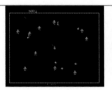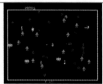

If you had to provide a representation of twitch gaming at its most intense, you'd be best advised to choose this, an absurdly busy shoot 'em up whose ability to race pulses is without equal. Extremely crude, its two-joystick control system fosters a relationship between man and machine unmatched by any other coin-op effort.

Secret of Monkey Island
048

Format: **PC**
Publisher: **Activision**
Developer: **LucasArts**
Date: **1990**

Edge issue: n/a

Point-and-click adventure which makes fabulous use of simple graphics to create memorable characters and atmospheric locations. But the story provides the laughs. Everyone has their favourite part, and like a classic film, it's timeless.

Ultima Online
047

Format: **PC**
Publisher: **Electronic Arts**
Developer: **Origin**
Date: **1997**

Edge issue: 54

Meridian 59 may have got there first but *Ultima Online* brings all of Origin's comprehensive understanding of roleplay gaming to the online scene. Open gameplay, a huge world and rich detail mark out this slab of 'virtual reality'.

R4: Ridge Racer Type 4
046

Format: **PlayStation**
Publisher: **Namco**
Developer: **In-house**
Date: **1999**

Edge issue: 68

The fourth instalment in Namco's popular arcade-styled racer combines its astounding technical aptitude with tried-and-tested *RR* gameplay mechanics. Not necessarily a game for *GT* lovers, *Type 4* is nevertheless an exhilarating drive.

Wave Race 64
045

Format: **N64**
Publisher: **Nintendo**
Developer: **In-house**
Date: **1996**

Edge issue: 39

1080° Snowboarding and *Wave Race* share an exceptional control system which makes them leader in respective genres. Again Nintendo's understanding of balanced structure and gameplay value results in a jawdropping game.

DAVID PERRY

PRESIDENT, SHINY ENTERTAINMENT

MY ALL-TIME FAVOURITES...

1. GoldenEye (N64) The team in Rare that made this game were obviously hardcore gamers that got a chance to make a game.
2. Wave Race 64 (N64) I love a simple (yet impressive) game that friends can play without a giant learning curve.
3. Tekken 3 (PS) Still my favourite fighting game.
4. Command & Conquer (PC) Time stood still when I first sat down to this game.
5. Jetpac (Spectrum) This was one of the first 'smooth movement' sprite games. It was also fun. (In those days.)
6. Sonic (Mega Drive) It was a real kick in the pants to everyone that thought they were making impressive Genesis titles.
7. Driver (PC) I like games that reward you for being a crazy-ass, not just for clinical driving.
8. Moon Cresta (coin-op) I used to love this machine as a kid.
9. Stunt Car Racer (Amiga) I loved it – a very dangerous track to be trying to race on. Took ages to perfect.
10. Populous (Amiga) Peter Molyneux making great new genres as usual.

044 Star Fox 64

Format: **N64**
Publisher: **Nintendo**
Developer: **In-house**
Date: **1997**

Edge issue: 46

The original had more impact in its realm, of course, but if you really want to experience the closest thing to taking part in 'Star Wars'-style dogfights, nothing emulates the sensation quite as expertly as this Miyamoto-produced 64bit update. As ever, there are plenty of hidden bonuses here to keep you powering up time and again.

043 Sega Rally

Format: **Coin-op**
Manufacturer: **Sega**
Developer: **In-house (AM3)**
Date: **1995**

Edge issue: 18

Tetsuya Mizuguchi's finest moment? There have been few games since which have conveyed the feeling of sliding a rally-spec car through beautifully rendered tracks with such aplomb. The coin-op version remains the most engaging.

042 Secret of Mana

Format: **SNES**
Publisher: **SquareSoft**
Developer: **In-house**
Date: **1993**

Edge issue: 04

Despite the obvious limitations of cartridges, their use can so often reveal the true potential within a developer, and rarely more so than with *Secret Of Mana*, one of the most beautifully crafted console games of the '90s. Graphics, music, story, gameplay, balance – the 16Mbit SNES cart conveys every element in a dreamlike manner.

041 1080° Snowboarding

Format: **N64**
Publisher: **Nintendo**
Developer: **In-house**
Date: **1998**

Edge issue: 57

Only let down by cheap AI routines, *1080°* often offers moments of pure videogaming magic. The feeling of surfing down the side of a mountain through various types of snow has yet to be captured with the same magnificence.

040 Hidden & Dangerous

Format: **PC**
Publisher: **Take Two Interactive**
Developer: **Illusion Software**
Date: **1999**

Edge issue: 73

The surprise PC hit of the year, *Hidden & Dangerous* drew on the best of *Commandos* and *Quake*. Too hard for some, its squad-based action manages to balance tactical decisions with tense gameplay in historically accurate missions.

039 X-Wing vs TIE Fighter

Format: **PC**
Publisher: **LucasArts**
Developer: **In-house**
Date: **1997**

Edge issue: 45

This combination of LucasArts flight shooters gets closer than any other 'Star Wars' licence to making the player feel a part of the film. Lacking in the singleplayer department, *X Wing vs Tie Fighter* is a multiplayer *tour de force*. For fans, getting together with friends and taking on an Imperial Star Destroyer is a near-religious experience.

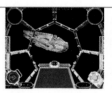 

038 Doom II

Format: **PC**
Publisher: **GT Interactive**
Developer: **Id Software**
Date: **1994**

Edge issue: 14

If any title cemented the PC's reputation as the extreme games machine, it was *Doom II*. More gory and more puzzling than the original, it proved both addictive and innovative, elevating head id coder John Carmack to genius status.

Bust-a-Move 2

037

Format: **PS**
Publisher: **Acclaim**
Developer: **Taito**
Date: **1996**

Edge issue: 34

Originally driven by SNK's Neo-Geo MVS, Taito doubtless did not know what it was starting when it unleashed the first *Puzzle Bobble*. Now, countless sequels and home versions later, the format has touched the lives of even the most unlikely looking videogamer. Confused by the number of versions out there? Plump for this one.

Colin McRae Rally

036

Format: **PS**
Publisher: **Codemasters**
Developer: **In-house**
Date: **1998**

Edge issue: 61

There were rally games before Codemasters' entry into the world of off-road competition, and several contenders since, but *Colin McRae Rally* still delivers the most accomplished mix of realism, excitement, structure and gameplay.

PilotWings 64

035

Format: **N64**
Publisher: **Nintendo**
Developer: **In-house/Paradigm**
Date: **1996**

Edge issue: 35

While the SNES original introduced the concept, it's this N64 successor that delivers the better game experience. *PilotWings 64* not only remains one of Nintendo's greatest creations but a stubbornly and marvellously different one, too.

International Track & Field

034

Format: **PS**
Publisher: **Konami**
Developer: **In-house**
Date: **1996**

Edge issue: 34

Tiresome for one player, but add a multitap and three joypads and *IT&F* becomes one of the most compulsively competitive videogames ever. The sight of four adults furiously jabbing at buttons even makes it a spectator sport, too.

Castlevania: Symphony of the Night

033

Format: **PS**
Publisher: **Konami**
Developer: **In-house**
Date: **1997**

Edge issue: 51

Not the most beautiful title to have graced Sony's 32bit machine, Konami's first and only PlayStation outing for its *Castlevania* series is a massively overlooked title that is beautifully balanced and extraordinarily engrossing. Hunt it down now.

Resident Evil

032

Format: **PS**
Publisher: **Capcom**
Developer: **In-house**
Date: **1996**

Edge issue: 33

Not as graphically accomplished as its sequels, the original *Resident Evil* still offers some of the most shocking experiences to videogamers, capturing the essence of classic horror flicks. The result is a frighteningly involving affair.

ISS Pro Evolution

031

Format: **PS**
Publisher: **Konami**
Developer: **In-house**
Date: **1999**

Edge issue: 80

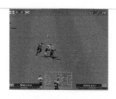

Convincing visuals, exceptional attention to detail, a wonderful control system, outstanding responsiveness, and unparalleled AI combine to make this the definitive football game from the world's master of the sport in digital form.

GARY PENN,

CREATIVE MANAGER, DMA DESIGN

MY ALL-TIME FAVOURITES…

Bomberman (PC Engine) I'm enamoured more by the basic rules and the toy itself than any specific exploitation. I guess the defining moment would be the original PC Engine version – accessible and fun for five players of any age, gender or ability.

Defender (coin-op) Apart from *Robotron* nothing comes close to *Defender*'s extreme demands for mental and physical dexterity and synchronicity. There's a steep learning curve but at the top awaits an exceptional reward: a distinctive hypnotic trip.

Doom (PC) There's no denying its lingering influence on style, content and production values on the PC. After this I lost all interest in contemporary interpretations of 'war with sticks for guns', like *Quake* and *Unreal*.

Elite (BBC) Undeniably a considered, powerful illusion of a 'living' universe – the first 'freeform' environment with focused set-pieces – and capable of suggesting so much to so many. It's always impressed me and yet bored me shitless at the same time.

Parappa the Rapper (PlayStation) 'But it's only Simon Says.' So what? What's done with the concept is always more important than the concept itself. Here is a delightful rarity which offers accessible, amiable fun for all the family.

Pokémon Blue/Red (Game Boy) Banal fantasy roleplaying with turn-based combat made entertaining and accessible to all. Staggering. Such a considered compendium – and such considered execution and delivery of the repertoire.

Populous (Amiga) I never enjoyed playing it that much but I can't help but admire its presence. It was a defining moment – an inspiring means of playing with digital toys – and it heralded a new pigeonhole: the god sim.

The Sentinel (C64) Abstract. Surreal. Atmospheric. Immersive. Challenging. Scary. Unique. (And *The Sentinel Returns* stank like rancid cheesy cabbage fish.)

Super Mario Bros It's the 'Mario Universe' – the toy set and its consistent, ingenious exploitation that's remarkable. But if push came to shove… Probably *3*. Or *World*. Or perhaps *64*.

Tetris (Game Boy) Oh, it seems so simple… but it's so easy to get the rules wrong and end up with an inept interpretation (as so many clones consistently demonstrate). It revolutionised the 'puzzler' and continues to inspire. It will live forever.

030 Soul Calibur

Format: **DC**
Publisher: **Namco**
Developer: **In-house**
Date: **1999**

Edge issue: 76

One of the few games to better its arcade parent, Dreamcast *Soul Calibur* is the most beautiful-looking beat 'em up ever conceived. Crucially, though, it supports its visual prowess with the usual gameplay values associated with a Namco production. Supremely balanced, and with an inordinate amount of oneplayer lifespan, too.

029 Starcraft

Format: **PC**
Publisher: **Sierra**
Developer: **Blizzard**
Date: **1998**

Edge issue: 59

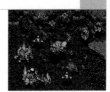

Taking the *Warcraft* legacy into space, Blizzard's RTS didn't have the most revolutionary control system, but the balance between the in-game three alien races is masterfully accomplished. The multiplayer still beats most of today's RTS games.

028 Tempest 2000

Format: **Jaguar**
Publisher: **Atari**
Developer: **Jeff Minter**
Date: **1994**

Edge issue: 08

The original arcade game, though still big on playability, fails to capture videogamers the way Minter's masterfully updated version does with its beautifully psychedelic visuals and whacked-out sound effects. Playability in undiluted form.

027 Anna Kournikova's Smash Court Tennis

Format: **PS**
Publisher: **Namco**
Developer: **In-house**
Date: **1999**

Edge issue: n/a

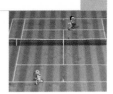

The latest member of Namco's *Smash Court* family (only rivalled by the SNES's *Super Tennis*) inherits all of its ancestors' playability. Matches between four able players deliver some of the most intense videogaming experiences around.

026 Sim City 2000

Format: **PC**
Publisher: **EA**
Developer: **Maxis**
Date: **1993**

Edge issue: 07

With double the map size, *Sim City 2000* is a good-looking game of almost unparalleled depth. In fact it's more of a Lego set combined with a town-planning tool. Lord knows how Maxis makes that combination work so well.

025 NiGHTS: Into Dreams

Format: **Saturn**
Publisher: **Sega**
Developer: **In-house (Sonic Team)**
Date: **1996**

Edge issue: 36

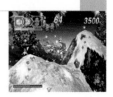

The game that should have saved the Saturn, *NiGHTS* is a beautiful and compelling experience, taking the fluid, trippy atmosphere of *Sonic* into a weird, hyper-colourful dream world. Wholly unorthodox, and better for it.

024 Final Fantasy Tactics

Format: **PS**
Publisher: **SquareSoft**
Developer: **In-house**
Date: **1998**

Edge issue: 57

For anyone who appreciates a more cerebral videogame challenge, Square's most notable console wargame is the hardcore gamer's choice. Not for those solely familiar with *FFVII* and its sequel, this is nevertheless pure class.

PAUL DAVIES

MR HARDCORE

MY ALL-TIME FAVOURITES…

NiGHTS
Final Fantasy VII
Tekken 3
Pac-Man
Ghouls 'n' Ghosts
Super Mario Kart
Street Fighter II
Gunstar Heroes
Pokémon
Super Mario World

These games are ones that I've been most obsessed about. I did my 4th year English 'talk' on **Pac-Man**, when I was 14. I almost lost my job at EMAP for all the **Tekken 3** coverage in *CVG* (true). I own lots of **Pokémon** music CDs… and listen to them! Tom Guise and I invented lyrics to go with the victory tunes to **Super Mario Kart**: 'Tommy is the best, there's no doubt about it, better than all the rest…' (for Luigi) '… nonetheless Tom-is-the-best' (and he is). We also based our life's philosophy on that game at the time. You know, you think you're ahead and you get too confident, then someone gets the proverbial lightning bolt and it's all over for you. (Some people get all the lightning bolts in life, and it's usually the losers.) I cried when Aerith died. I cry every time I think about how beautiful the message for kids is in **NiGHTS**, though I expect that kids think it's a load of crap. I know where every chest is in **Ghouls 'n' Ghosts**. I conducted many important discussions about the team with my editor, Andy McVittie, when we did *Nintendo Magazine*. And that bit at the end of **Gunstar Heroes** where Green refuses to fight Red and Blue… my god, how awesome was that! And I don't want to tell you what **Super Mario World** means to me – that's probably scary/boring/irrelevant.

X-Com: Enemy Below
023

Format: **PC**
Publisher: **Microprose**
Developer: **In-house**
Date: **1985**

Edge issue: n/a

Building on the impressive foundations of the original turn-based strategy shooter, this version adds tougher enemies and larger more visually appealing environments to create a game the likes of which we will probably never see again.

GP2
022

Format: **PC**
Publisher: **Microprose**
Developer: **Geoff Crammond**
Date: **1996**

Edge issue: 31

Grand Prix was excellent. *Grand Prix 2* is astounding. Still without equal (presumably *Grand Prix 3* may give it a run for its money), *GP2* has consistently remained ahead of fierce competition when it comes to F1 sims.

Total Annihilation
021

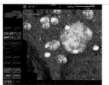

Format: **PC**
Publisher: **GT Interactive**
Developer: **Cavedog**
Date: **1997**

Edge issue: 52

The blueprint laid down by *Command & Conquer* and stretched in every direction. True 3D backgrounds allow players hide behind hills, and the 150 units, 50 singleplayer missions and massive online support make it a classic.

Tomb Raider
020

Format: **PS**
Publisher: **Eidos**
Developer: **Core Design**
Date: **1996**

Edge issue: 40

Tomb Raider: The Last Revelation may be more technically sound, but none of the successors match the astonishment felt in the original as a new room was unveiled, a rock facade scaled or a highly dangerous dive accomplished.

Tekken 3
019

Format: **PS**
Publisher: **Namco**
Developer: **In-house**
Date: **1998**

Edge issue: 58

As the most complete package in Namco's standard-setting beat 'em up series, *Tekken 3* is a lesson in playability. Irrespective of the developer's technical achievements, the game offers supremely crafted gameplay and like all *Tekkens* is both accessible to newcomers and can still represent a real challenge to veterans.

Super Mario Kart
018

Format: **SNES**
Publisher: **Nintendo**
Developer: **In-house**
Date: **1992**

Edge issue: n/a

The N64 version may have its supporters, but when all is said and done, it fails to stand up to the majesty of the 16bit original. Yes, CPU-controlled drivers cheat like nobody's business, but that simply makes the experience all the more compulsive, and ultimately rewarding. Twoplayer sessions are delights to savour.

Super Bomberman
017

Format: **SNES**
Publisher: **HudsonSoft**
Developer: **In-house**
Date: **1994**

Edge issue: n/a

Ignore the sequels, which try too hard to add novel touches and ruin what was an already near-flawless structure. Fourplayer *Bomberman* is magnificently frantic, free-for-all gaming built from the ground up with ingenious mechanics.

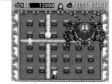

DEMIS HASSABIS

CEO, ELIXIR STUDIOS

MY ALL-TIME FAVOURITES...

1. Civilisation (PC) My favourite game of all time. Embodies the 'just one more turn' edict. Absolutely seminal.

2. Elite (BBC) Its vision still hasn't been equalled. Way before its time and an incredible achievement.

3. Carrier Command (Amiga) Diverse and fearlessly original. The balance of strategy and action was perfect and the AI impressive.

4. Dungeon Master (Amiga) Great design. Immersive with incredible depth, before its time.

5. Populous (Amiga) Created a whole genre. One of the most original games of all time.

6. Speedball (Amiga) My favourite sports game and probably the most instantly playable game ever.

7. Rebelstar (Spectrum) The forerunner to *Laser Squad* and then the *X-COM* series. Superb gameplay and balance. Inspirational.

8. Doom (PC) One of the best multiplayer games ever. A phenomenal landmark game.

9. Stunt Car Racer (Amiga) Most fun and imaginative racing game ever. Superb in single player, even better with two.

10. M.U.L.E. (C64) A quirky game, nevertheless one of the coolest of its time. Fantastic gameplay in multiplayer.

016 Metal Gear Solid

Format: **PS**
Publisher: **Konami**
Developer: **In-house**
Date: **1998**

First previewed in **E**46, Hideo Kojima's stealth masterpiece is the most convincing example of how close a videogame can get to Hollywood's finest while matching its narrative with superlative gameplay. Technically flawless, visually arresting, never anything less than thoroughly engrossing, and still surprising players until the very last 'level', *Metal Gear Solid* is an experience that only fully reveals itself to players prepared to take their time with it. Solid stuff indeed.

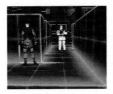

Edge issue: 64

015 Super Puyo Puyo

Format: **SNES**
Publisher: **Banpresto**
Developer: **Compile**
Date: **1994**

Edge issue: 07

After *Tetris*, the race was on to take the proven falling-blocks concept, give it a spin, and hope for dear life to somehow replicate its magic. The only truly convincing example is this, a blob-strewn affair with manic twoplayer gameplay.

014 Super Metroid

Format: **SNES**
Publisher: **Nintendo**
Developer: **In-house**
Date: **1994**

There has rarely been a finer illustration of balanced gameplay dynamics than in Gumpei Yokoi's scarily immersive SNES adventure. And few games have either proved as rewarding or as effective in driving players forwards and left them with such feelings of emptiness upon completion. *Super Metroid* has a timeless quality only videogaming's elite will ever enjoy. In a world of polygons and three dimensions, this 2D scrolling adventure puts most of today's videogames to shame.

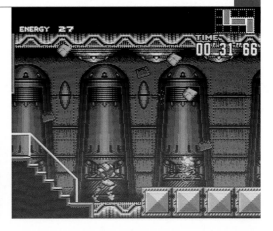

Edge issue: 09

013 Final Fantasy VII

Format: **PS**
Publisher: **SquareSoft**
Developer: **In-house**
Date: **1997**

Likely candidate for the title greatest RPG ever, *Final Fantasy VII* brought the delights of quirky Japanese gaming into the western mainstream. Massive in size and capricious in its random battles, it wasn't an easy game to get into, but more than rewarded those who waded through the first few hours. The complexity of characters such as Aeris, Cloud and Sephiroth has yet to be matched, and more tears have been shed over its twisting, emotionally laden story than any other game.

Edge issue: 51

Civilisation 2

012

Format: **PC**
Publisher: **Microprose**
Developer: **In-house**
Date: **1996**

Never before, and rarely since, has a game offered such depth, such staggering detail and such incredible historical accuracy. *Civilisation 2* takes the foundations of the first game, provides a graphical overhaul and adds dozens of technologies and units – expanding a fascinating idea into an engrossing epic. There are so many possibilities, so many different ways to play, this is a truly timeless work. As Samuel Johnson might have said, a man who is tired of *Civilisation 2* is tired of life.

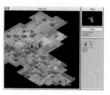 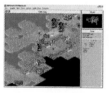

Edge issue: 32

Pokémon

011

Format: **GB**
Publisher: **Nintendo**
Developer: **Game Freak**
Date: **1996**

A triumph of the synergy between hardware and software, the *Pokémon* phenomenon now rules the world. Its mixture of Tamagotchi training and RPG adventure is as sophisticated as anything on 'proper' consoles. Nintendo's biggest hit?

Edge issue: n/a

Super Mario World

010

Format: **SNES**
Publisher: **Nintendo**
Developer: **In-house**
Date: **1991**

The dawn of 16bit Nintendo technology needed something special in software terms to drive it, and, without the merest whiff of surprise, Shigeru Miyamoto and his team of obscenely talented engineers at NCL HQ were the ones to provide it. Graphics are functional yet consummately effective. Audio is typically twee. Gameplay? Gameplay is astonishing, engrossing, bewilderingly addictive. Any gamer who hasn't conquered *Super Mario World*'s 96 levels hasn't lived.

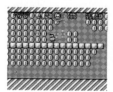 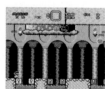

Edge issue: n/a

Half-Life

009

Format: **PC**
Publisher: **Sierra/Havas**
Developer: **Valve**
Date: **1998**

Despite using borrowed engine code (albeit substantially tweaked) This epoch-shattering firstperson shooter does something no id title has ever really achieved, providing a thrilling and densely plotted singleplayer mode. Guiding Gordon Freeman through the flickering corridors, sludgy air vents, and echoing mining tunnels of the Black Mesa complex is an unforgettable ride. And the multiplayer options are fantastic, too. On this evidence, Valve may yet conquer the PC gaming world.

Edge issue: 66

008 Street Fighter II Turbo

Format: **Coin-op/SNES**
Publisher: **Capcom**
Developer: **In-house**
Date: **1993**

In arcade or SNES incarnation, still the king of beat 'em ups, despite the graphical frippery that has since been thrown around by the likes of Namco and Sega. A game of such apparent simplicity, but underneath everything one of the deepest experiences ever burned on to silicon, *Street Fighter II Turbo* is a Zen-like experience. Like *Quake II*, this is videogaming as a sport whenever multiplayer sessions are indulged. Did Capcom realise what a durable title it was creating back in the early '90s? Because this will still be played in ten years' time.

Edge issue: 01

007 The Legend of Zelda: A Link to the Past

Format: **SNES**
Publisher: **Nintendo**
Developer: **In-house**
Date: **1992**

Parts one and two on the NES were mere tasters for what was to come – although few could have expected instalment number three to be so preposterously engaging. Looked at from a design perspective, this is little short of a miracle, its countless components fitting together like some fantastical jigsaw in videogame form. Two particular marks of genius stand out – the relationship which exists between the Light and the Dark worlds, and the way your character grows as the adventure progresses – but everything in here is made of gold.

Edge issue: n/a

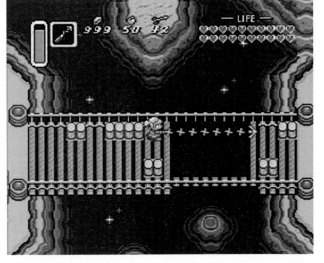

006 Quake II

Format: **PC**
Publisher: **Activision**
Developer: **Id Software**
Date: **1997**

Wolfenstein started it all, *Doom* tweaked it, and *Quake* brought true 3D. But it was *Quake II* that premiered advanced physics, complex AI, realtime lighting, ambient sound and, perhaps most important of all, 32-player online combat. It remains the most played deathmatch title in existence, chiefly because everything is so perfectly, artistically, intellectually balanced. Those who criticise the average singleplayer mode are missing the point – *Quake II* is meant to be shared, it's a culture in itself. A copy of John Carmack's code should be on exhibition in the Tate.

Edge issue: 54

Gran Turismo 2

005

Format: **PS**
Publisher: **SCE**
Developer: **Polyphony Digital Inc**
Date: **1999**

A staggering selection of vehicles, superb track design, sublime structure, peerless technical aptitude, revolutionary dynamics, unprecedented level of realism, superior longevity and an unparalleled sense of immersion powered *Gran Turismo* into the all-time greats videogaming circuit. Amazingly, not only does the sequel improve on every aspect of its astounding predecessor but also manages to bring new elements of its own into the mix, making this the most complete, most engrossing and thoroughly convincing racing videogame the world has ever seen.

Edge issue: 81

Tetris

004

Format: **GB**
Publisher: **Bulletproof Software**
Developer: **In-house**
Date: **1989**

Reputedly the game that every coder wishes he'd 'knocked up in an afternoon', you can be sure that, even if the concept of slotting falling geometric shapes into a tidy pile at the base of the playing area had occurred to someone other than Alexey Pajitnov while they were having a soak in the bath, the result would not have been so convincingly rounded as how *Tetris* turned out. And that's the genius of it – the number of pieces available seems spot on, the size of the 'well' feels perfect… everything just feels so *right*. Sheer brilliance.

Edge issue: n/a

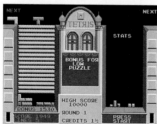
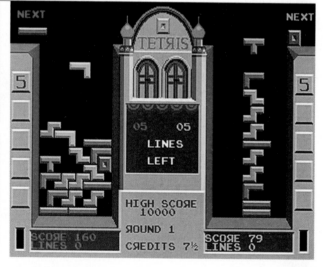

GoldenEye

003

Format: **N64**
Publisher: **Nintendo**
Developer: **Rare**
Date: **1997**

When it was released some 28 months ago, *GoldenEye* revolutionised the firstperson-perspective genre. Until then, *Doom* clones were just that – brainless, albeit enjoyable, action fests with every release upping the graphical ante. But Rare's offering boasted a highly realistic, detailed setting while rewarding players prepared to use a little intelligence and a cautious approach when completing the inspirationally designed levels' objectives. One or two contenders may have come very close, but the resulting sense of immersion has not been equalled since.

Edge issue: 48

002 Super Mario 64

Format: **N64**
Publisher: **Nintendo**
Developer: **In-house**
Date: **1996**

As **Edge** said in issue 76 (when looking at the games attempting to follow in Nintendo's carefully considered 3D footsteps), upon entering *Super Mario 64* for the first time, every previous *Mario* game suddenly looks like a postcard from this place. Its vibrancy is almost tangible; it feels alive in a technicolour hyper-real sense.

The subtle sound of chirping of birds and the sight of flittering butterflies as you take your first tentative, analogue-driven steps in Mario's new universe serve to captivate gamers as toy shop windows do children in the run up to Christmas. Where *Ocarina of Time* struggles to offer a welcome mat with its opening sequence, walking away from *Super Mario 64* once you've made the little plumber leap and 'yahoo!' his way across the grassy plain towards Bowser's castle is simply not an option.

As *World* had before it, *64* took a fresh set of tools and used them to build a brave new world whose boundaries seemed almost limitless. Accessing each new area was a genuine thrill, as the promise of more exploration loomed. What was through that door in the sunken ship? How can that grill in the moat be reached? What are these pink-hued panels dotted about the place for? Finding the answers to every question is an ineffably compulsive pursuit.

Being broken down into such distinct chunks has brought criticisms of the game, but this structure allowed *Super Mario 64*'s designers to create a selection of the most diverse environments imaginable. Granted, sand, lava, snow and ice are hardly the most groundbreaking elements, but in this context they feel as fresh as an autumn breeze.

An adventure playground in digital form comprising the most wildly entertaining attractions imaginable, this is the best videogame of all time. Almost.

Edge issue: 35

Legend of Zelda: Ocarina of Time

Format: **N64**
Publisher: **Nintendo**
Developer: **In-house**
Date: **1998**

Nintendo-produced games may take longer to gestate than those from any other company (and the implications of this will have serious repercussions on the company's future), but it could never be said that they're not worth the wait.

The company had already earned its wings in the polygon-crazy era of the mid-to-late-'90s with Mario's 64bit adventure, but taking Link, a character whose existence has always depended on something more than deftly jumping on opponents' heads for success, and reinterpreting every element of his world in 3D was a task which bore comparison to reinventing the wheel.

When NCL's design teams congregate to chew over ideas and put together viable design concepts, they use vast office walls upon which they place scores of Post-It notes bearing scribbled ideas. They then mix and match individual elements until coherent, flowing structures appear. Like brainstorms conducted over pints of bitter in a pub, it is a low-tech approach to a crucially consequential aspect of the design process, and Nintendo must have kept a Kyoto stationer very happy during the three years that it took to bring *Ocarina of Time* from scraps of paper to the single most impressive slice of videogaming the world has ever had the joy of witnessing.

Perhaps Nintendo's biggest achievement here is in creating a believable world, a collection of locations unimpeded by CD access and FMV cut scenes, brought together with a sense of cohesion that makes it the ultimate slice of fantasy 'virtual reality'.

Ocarina of Time wasn't supposed to be this good, of course. Production delays suggest one thing more than any other: problems. But, with the assistance of the most humble of office stationery items, NCL succeeded in creating a game that will always be remembered as the stuff of legend.

Edge issue: 66

VIDEOGAMING:
THE ODYSSEY

As the world prepares to welcome a new wave of technology with open arms, **Edge** takes a trip back through time, reeling in the hardware that made videogaming the cultural phenomenon it is today

T hough it has only recently gained real acceptance as an entertainment device of worth to match the television, satellite dish and VCR, the videogame console was conceived in the US in the late-'60s.

In the 30 years since, literally hundreds of leisure-enhancing gaming devices have passed through bedrooms and living rooms as the march of technology ensured obsolescence was a built-in consideration for these boxes of consumer electronics.

Over the next 11 pages, Edge celebrates this march, remembering the videogame consoles and home computers that have touched so many lives so deeply.

Every machine featured here has its historical relevance, whether it's Magnavox's Odyssey (opposite), which offered analogue controllers fashioned with a faux-wood veneer (a nod towards acceptance in the living room a quarter of a century before Sony decided to give its PlayStation2 the design values of a piece of hi-fi equipment), the Atari 400 (with its four joystick ports as standard), or Sinclair's ZX80 (whose appearance marked the beginning of Britain's – albeit brief – spell as a hardware-designing force to be reckoned with).

Their relevance today? Consider this: a mint-condition Magnavox Odyssey can now change hands for over £1,000. What was once the most primitive example of videogame hardware has come to earn museum status. It's something to keep in mind the next time you're clearing out the attic.

Magnavox Odyssey

While the rest of American youth were experimenting with free love and hallucinogenic drugs, two young engineers, Bill Arrison and Bill Rusley, under the guidance of development manager Ralph Baer, began work on what would become the world's first videogame console. The year was 1966, and by 1967 they had created a fully operational prototype. It took a further three years to license the machine to television manufacturer Magnavox. The Odyssey, as it was eventually named, was very expensive to produce, comprising over 300 components, and capable of displaying only three dots on screen simultaneously. Lack of colour and sound was compensated for by the inclusion of bright screen overlays, and additional board games. The Odyssey's 1972 launch was relatively successful, shipping just over 100,000 units by 1975. Shortly after Atari released *Pong*, Magnavox sued Atari, stating that Bushnell had stolen the idea for the game after viewing a prototype of the Odyssey. Atari emerged unharmed and went on to sell over 150,000 of its home *Pong* machines.

Odyssey carts (left) were card-like in construction. Six came packed in with the unit.
A plastic overlay (right) was used with each game in an attempt to liven up visuals

When it all began, audio was blips and graphics blobs, but the '70s saw gaming hardware begin to get into its stride

Fairchild Channel F   1976

Fairchild's Channel F may look like an old eight-track cartridge player, but in 1976 it represented the state of the art in videogame entertainment. Simple versions of *Hockey* and *Tennis* came supplied on the Channel F's internal ROM, and Fairchild committed itself to releasing a new game for the machine every month. During its lifespan, 27 cartridges were released, including groundbreaking titles such as the educational *MathQuiz,* and art title *Doodle.*

Bally Arcade   1976

The original Bally Professional Arcade was released in 1976 and quickly established itself as the first computer/console hybrid. Unusually, the most popular cartridge for the machine was its *BASIC* cartridge, which allowed users to write programs in the console's 4K RAM, and save them to cassette. Many gamers were attracted to the machine, too, thanks to its built-in version of the arcade classic, *Boot Hill.* The huge success of Atari's VCS forced Bally to cease production of the console in 1979, although the story doesn't end there: a group of enthusiasts bought the rights to the machine from Bally and re-released the console as the Astrocade in 1981, including the *BASIC* cartridge code built into the machine's ROM.

Atari Pong   1976

One of a trio of standalone units Atari released in the mid-'70s, *Pong* took the coin-op concept and transferred it lock, stock and barrel into the home. The unit's chief restriction was its immovable controllers, presumably incorporated in this fashion in order to make the console experience as close as possible to the arcade original. Coleco delivered a *Pong* clone at around the same time, and both companies enjoyed enormous success, shifting several million units worldwide.

Atari Video Pinball   1977

Like *Pong* and *Stunt Bike*, *Video Pinball* was a dedicated Atari unit which featured controls built as part of the console (making it an unwieldy beast), and at a time when gamers would buy just about anything so long as it bore an Atari badge, it enjoyed no small amount of success. The company eventually turned the three titles into self-contained units for its Game Brain initiative, now one of the rarest machines on the collector's circuit.

Magnavox Odyssey 2   1978

The second experiment into console hardware from Dutch electronics giant Philips, the Odyssey 2 was released in Europe as the Videopac G7000. With a touch-sensitive (some would say thump-sensitive) keyboard as standard, it was supposed to appeal to adults seeking to give their children something more than a 'mere' games machine. In the absence of wide-scale software support, however, the console was always destined to come off second best to Atari's all-conquering VCS.

Atari VCS/2600

The machine that made videogaming as a hobby in the home, and a fortune for Atari, the VCS (Video Computer System) also brought about the console crash of the early '80s. Because it was so easy to develop for (90 per cent of its games were created as one-person projects),

a surfeit of under-par titles swamped the format, eventually resulting in consumer apathy. In its heyday, however, the VCS attracted the biggest names, playing host to licences from the likes of Namco and Taito, and gave birth to one of today's most powerful third parties, Activision.

Atari 400

By the end of the '70s Atari had decided to refocus its efforts into producing a range of computers. When released in 1979 the Atari 400 offered hi-resolution, colour graphics, and three-channel sound. However, due to its small memory (16K) and limited touch-sensitive keyboard, its

bigger, 64K brother, the 800, accumulated more sales. A comparatively high price and VCS incompatibility let the Apple][steal a march on the home-computing sector in the US. Intriguingly, however, the 400 and 800 offered four joystick ports as standard. How's that for being there first?

Ingersoll TV Game

The success of *Pong* led to a deluge of TV games. By the late -'70s there were over 50 companies building simple non-cartridge machines, including Radofin and Binatone. Most TV games were based on the same range of chips, courtesy of

General Instruments – the wide use of its AY-38500 chip meant there was often little to distinguish one machine from another. This Ingersoll R-1800 is worthy of note thanks to its spherical controllers and offensively orange casing.

Mattel Intellivision

Toy company Mattel felt obliged to grab a slice of the console market as it burgeoned in the late '70s. The result was a machine more sophisticated than Atari's VCS, with graphics of a higher resolution, and even an optional speech module.

However, in designing the Intellivision, Mattel also created the world's first console joypad, a 'rockable disc' affair which alienated some users who equated videogames with joysticks. Despite this, the machine enjoyed some fine software.

Sinclair ZX80

Having enjoyed success as a pioneer of calculators and digital watches in the consumer electronics market, Clive Sinclair gave birth to his first personal computer in 1980. Despite offering a smidgen less than 1K of onboard memory, and a lack of

graphics beyond simplistic blocks, the machine soon found favour with the type of hobbyists and electronics enthusiasts that keep Maplins in business today. It's no coincidence that Sinclair sold more ZX80s in kit form than ready assembled.

Now that Atari had successfully blazed a trail, the early '80s saw hardware design and production shift into top gear

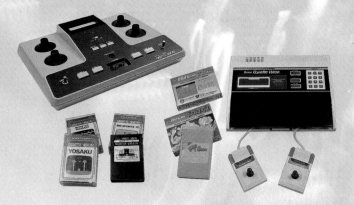

Epoch Cassette Vision/ Super Cassette Vision

Before Nintendo set foot in the hazard-strewn world of console production, Japanese company Epoch had the market pretty much to itself. Its first machine, the Cassette Vision, was a cartridge-based console with no external controllers; instead players manipulated onscreen action via four analogue paddles on the front of the console. The Cassette Vision enjoyed considerable success in Japan, outselling imports of the Atari VCS. When Nintendo finally showed its hand with the 1983 release of the Famicom, Epoch launched an updated version entitled the Super Cassette Vision. While relatively unsuccessful, Epoch's machine featured a similar specification to Nintendo unit, and games licensed from Taito.

Sega SC3000H

Sega released three different machines before the Master System. First was the SG1000, a simple, cartridge-based console released in Japan in 1981. Poor sales led to development of the SG3000 console, compatible with a wealth of hardware peripherals, including a steering wheel and keyboard. Finally the Sega Mark 3 filled the gap between the 3000 and Master System. Its games were delivered on cards, and are compatible with the Master System Mk1 via a slot in the machine's front. The SC3000H was an all-in-one computer version of the Japanese console, developed solely for Australasia.

Sinclair ZX81/ZX Spectrum

A year after the ZX80, the ZX81 became the first massmarket computer to hit the UK. Its 1K memory could be easily upgraded to 16K, and early software houses such as Quicksilva provided simple coin-op conversions and adventure games. Sinclair managed to sell over a million machines in the first year of production. By the end of the ZX81's brief lifespan, the ingenuity of British programming was beginning to shine through, achieving the impossible: hi-res graphics. The following year, with limited colours, tinny sound from an internal speaker, and a cassette loading system as standard, the ZX Spectrum went head to head with the Commodore 64. At half its rival's price, and significantly more accessible from a home coding perspective, the Spectrum enjoyed phenomenal success, selling over five million units and surviving as a viable format for over ten years, from jerky interpretations of *Scramble* and *Galaxian* in 1982, to smooth conversions of *Street Fighter II* and *Sim City* in 1992. As a breeding ground for UK coding talent, there is no more significant machine.

Texas Instruments TI-99/4A

Another calculator company seeking a taste of the home computing boom, Texas Instruments released this format to a largely unreceptive audience. Despite its impressive specs (cart compatibility, speech synthesis, three-channel sound plus white noise), the TI-99/4A's Pascal-based OS repelled large-scale support.

Commodore VIC-20/C64

It may have generated graphics using pixels like house bricks, but Commodore's 3.5K VIC-20 was more than a match for its competitors when it launched in 1981, not least because of its full keyboard. Always destined to play second fiddle to Sinclair's machines in terms of popularity, the machine was complemented in 198X by a more potent machine, the C64, with its positively 'elephantine' 64K of RAM. In the 8bit computer wars, if the Spectrum was the everyman's PlayStation, then the C64 was the N64 – something of a luxury, with slicker but more expensive games.

Emerson Arcadia

Despite being released in 1982, the Arcadia relied on '70s technology to drive its games. Its library of 23 cartridges contains no titles worthy of note, just simple interpretations of games from earlier systems. The Arcadia relied largely on its aesthetics to gain customer appeal, but the misguided use of tight telephone wire between the console and controllers meant players usually tugged the machine around the floor during use. A very similar machine was released in Europe under the guise of the Grundig Interton.

CBS Colecovision 1982

Any gamer wanting to seriously impress friends in the early '80s had little choice but to plump for this, the first machine to be marketed as being capable of bringing the quality of the arcade into the home.

A close (but not perfect, as was routinely claimed) conversion of *Donkey Kong* wowed Saturday afternoon shoppers in Dixons, but at £150 the console was never as accessible as Atari's VCS.

Acorn BBC/Electron 1982 | 83

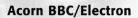

The spod's format of choice, the BBC series drew phenomenal attention from the education system thanks to its intelligent design and the Beeb's corporate endorsement, but it granted

users a wealth of legendary software, including, most famously, *Elite*. The Electron, its sawn-off little brother, turned up under the Christmas tree of many an unhappy kid who'd pined for a C64.

Camputers Lynx 1982

It wasn't enough that it came from a company with perhaps the most unintentionally amusing name in the home computing world; the Lynx was also overpriced, which ensured it would never

sell in numbers big enough to generate major software support. A Z80A-driven machine, its RAM could be expanded to 192K, an unheard-of figure in early-'80s computing in the home.

Oric 1 1982

Powered by a 6502A CPU, this was the Spectrum's most serious rival before the C64 gained a foothold. With a keyboard like pieces of Wrigley's Extra (or Beech Nut, as the comparison would have been

in 1982), this was a truly unconventional machine (its version of *BASIC* even offered ZAP and PING commands to generated sound effects). Its successor, the Atmos, did little to sell the Oric brand.

Dragon 32 1982

Released by Welsh company Dragon Data, this was intended to be a serious rival to the machines of Sinclair and Commodore, but its unconventional 6809E CPU and analogue joystick ports ensured it only a marginal presence throughout its relatively short lifespan. Dragon 32 users quickly became acclimatised to the machine's predilection for the colour green, a hue

that was to give the format's software a distinctive, if somewhat nausea-inducing, edge, but software support was not nearly as reliable. Microdeal, one company extremely committed to the machine, released a bundle of cynically conceived clones starring Cuthbert, one of computer gaming's least likable heroes.

Jupiter Ace 1982

Conceived by two ex-Sinclair Research employees, Steven Vickers and Richard Altwasser, the Ace was always destined to forage for attention while higher profile formats were simply granted it by default.

Eschewing *BASIC* in favour of *FORTH* proved a fundamental error, as the great unwashed was in the process of accepting Beginner's All-Purpose Instruction Set as its native computer tongue at this point.

Mattel Aquarius 1983

Using a tweaked version of Mattel's Intellivision technology, the Aquarius offered some interesting software on cart, but thirdparty coders dismissed it, making it possibly the most unsupported of all home computer formats. Expansion

modules and planned CP/M support simply highlighted Mattel's inexperience in the field. But the company pressed on, designing two more iterations of the hardware, neither of which would ever make it to market.

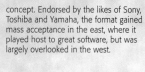

JVC MSX

It was the unlikely form of controller specialist Spectravideo that, along with Microsoft's Japanese arm, attempted to introduce a home computing standard with the MSX (MicroSoft eXtended) concept. Endorsed by the likes of Sony, Toshiba and Yamaha, the format gained mass acceptance in the east, where it played host to great software, but was largely overlooked in the west.

MB Vectrex

The most innovative console to come out of the '80s, Milton Bradley's all-in-one monochrome console was the preserve of the more specialist gamer, who understood that a lack of sprites simply served to make this an intriguing platform.

Like some other gaming technologies before it, the Vectrex used acetate screen overlays as a token gesture towards bringing colour to its games, which included *Armour Attack*, *Scramble*, and the synthesised speech-laden *Spike*.

Sharp MZ700

Like its bigger brother, the MZ80a, Sharp's machine offered a number of extras built-in as standard, but it had an enormously difficult time convincing its target audience (families and parents who sought to 'balance their cheque book' using the 'wonders of computing technology') that it was a platform with a future. Nevertheless, the machine was pushed hard by clueless department store assistants, who conveniently failed to mention its lack of development support.

Amstrad CPC464

After its success in the budget hi-fi sector, it was little surprise when Alan Michael Sugar Trading (Amstrad) introduced a computer whose sole intention was to grab market share from Commodore and Sinclair. Despite its relative expense (a factor brought about because the machine was compatible only with dedicated monitors, mono or colour versions of which came bundled), Amstrad's machine, later followed by the likes of the 6128, swiftly became a huge success.

Atari 800XL

In 1984 Atari relaunched its range of computers with the 800/1200XL machines. While the restyling and improved keyboard were welcomed, it was the new lower price which created an increase in sales, albeit not dramatic.

Memotech MTX512

Following its success in the 8bit peripherals market, supplying add-ons for the ZX81 and Spectrum among others, this was Memotech's largely unsuccessful bid to carve out a niche of its own with a stylish, impressively specced unit. In the face of dominance by the big three, this became just one more format for the bin.

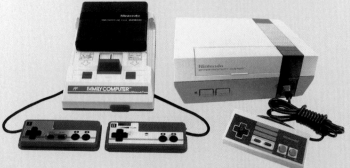

Nintendo Famicom/ Entertainment System

Consumers knew videogame class even in the early- to mid-'80s, and it was Shigeru Miyamoto software such as *Super Mario Bros* that made Nintendo's 8bit platform a phenomenon, not the technology itself. In the face of Sega's better-marketed Master System, the format did not explode in the UK, but in the territories that really mattered to Nintendo, Japan and the US, there was simply no stopping it. Despite attempting to give the console a shot in the arm with an ill-conceived Japan-only disc storage system, Nintendo did little wrong, and its lucrative licensing agreements ensured the company's profits swelled to titanic proportions.

By this point in the evolution of home computers and consoles, amazingly, some lessons still had not been learned

Sinclair QL   1986

In 1986 Sinclair introduced the world's first 16bit home computer. However, in a grave error of judgement, instead of aiming the machine at the installed

Spectrum userbase, Sinclair pushed the QL as a business machine, a decision which initiated the eventual demise of Sinclair home computers.

Atari 65XE   1987

The existence of the 65XE still now rather beggars belief. It must be assumed that Atari sought to offer videogamers a taste of home computing several rungs down from its ST series of the same era, but this market was already in rapid decline. As a gaming system the machine was in competition with the company's own

7800 console; as a computer it was hideously under-specced. It was in ploughing millions into launching products such as this that Atari showed tangible signs of losing the plot. Coleco's Adam system had famously proved that console/computer hybrids could not work, but no one at Atari had apparently noticed.

NEC PC Engine/TurboGrafx   1986|88

NEC's first venture into the console hardware market was simply magnificent. Its absurdly diminutive machine quickly became the more serious Japanese gamer's hardware of choice, and it was the format upon which the grey import

scene was built in the UK. With a custom 8bit CPU under the hood, 64 hardware sprites, and support from some of Japan's most innovative codeshops, it was little surprise to see the format become *the* format of choice among connoisseurs.

Amiga A500   1988

The darling of the 16bit home computer scene, the A500 was the accessible face of the Amiga world following the A1000.

Going up against Atari's ST range proved a difficult battle at first, but massive success ensured that machines are still in use today.

Sharp Famicom Twin   1988

Sales of the 1988 Sharp Famicom Twin cannot do justice to the historical significance of the machine. This was the first and only occasion Nintendo licensed its hardware to a thirdparty manufacturer, and its lack of success may well have

some relevance to the company's abandonment of Sony's CD version of the Super Famicom. The Twin is simply a Famicom and Famicom Disk System lumped together in one case, with a new operating system thrown in.

Amstrad GX4000   1990

Released in 1990 with virtually no software support, Amstrad's console was virtually ignored even from the day it was released. Similar to Commodore's C64-

based GS console, it is either a brave or ill-advised company that would choose to pitch an 8bit console against the might of the Mega Drive and Super Nintendo.

Sega Master System/SMSII   1986

Distributed by Virgin Mastertronic when it hit the UK, the Master System's 8bit architecture was comparable to Nintendo's NES, and Sega did its best in attempting to supply the machine with software to match the likes of *Super Mario Bros*. System sales kept up a good head of steam, resulting in a number of UK publishers jumping on board, until its 16bit Mega Drive successor arrived.

Mega Drive/Mega Drive 2   1988

Mainstream America had long since fallen back in love with the console concept thanks to the NES, but it wasn't until the Mega Drive arrived that UK households really began to clutch the concept to its bosom. Easily accessible software such as *FIFA*, *NHL* and *Sonic* helped, while Sega's marketing campaign projected the kind of cool sensibilities that it has only recently revisited with its DC campaign.

SNK Neo-Geo   1990

If you really want to know whether or not you're a hardcore gamer, there's a simple test: have you ever owned a piece of hardware with an SNK logo on it? (No, the Neo-Geo Pocket Color doesn't count.) Way ahead of its time, the Neo-Geo brought true coin-op power to the home – at a price of £200 per game.

Super Famicom/SNES   1990

Despite trailing Sega's 16bit hardware to market by nearly two years, it didn't take Nintendo long to claw back market share. Its supremely capable SNES took Japan by storm thanks to software from Shigeru Miyamoto's teams within NCL and thirdparty developers such Enix and SquareSoft, and its PAL iteration, though dogged by non-optimised 50Hz releases (and DC owners think *they* have it bad), slowly overtook the Mega Drive to become the dominant 16bit console.

NO CONSOLATION

The hardware showcased elsewhere in this feature at least had a chance to live or die. Spare a thought for these…

Whether they exist purely in the minds of over-eager technicians, on the drawing boards of pent-up designers, or in actual prototype form, certain games machines are destined to remain at the conceptual stage. These consoles are the most famous examples of just that.

Atari 'JagDuo'   1995

Shown at the 1995 summer CES in Chicago, this console was to be an all-in-one Jaguar-and-CD-drive unit. With Sony's PlayStation already available by this point, however, it didn't take Atari long to realise that such a format was dead in the water.

Sony PlayStation   early-'90s

With Nintendo supplying the guts, all it needed was Sony to supply CD-ROM storage technology and the happy alliance would be sealed. Except one company did not have faith in optical storage, leaving the other to take the concept on its own…

3DO M2 Series

Having summarily failed in his bid to deliver a format that would be a standard that would be to videogame hardware what VHS was to VCRs, Trip Hawkins pressed on with a new generation with M2. Result? A bunch of mere mockups.

1995

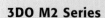

The most ambitious of ages, albeit one tainted by the ill-conceived promises of the 'multimedia revolution'

Fujitsu FM Towns Marty   1991

A little brother to the super-expensive FM Towns, the Marty used CD storage as standard, which alone created a heady air of excitement around the machine. However, in Japan it merely attracted hobbyist users, and despite – or perhaps because of – playing host to Psygnosis' *Microcosm*, one of the first FMV-driven console games, it attracted little interest here on import. Something of a curio, then.

Philips CD-i   1991

As a pioneer of the compact disc revolution, it was little surprise to see Philips make such bold strides in the pursuit of the format's potential outside of the audio realm. And how unfortunate it was to see the company deliver technology so patently incapable of doing justice to that potential. Even playing host to a series of *Zelda*-themed titles (somehow licensed from Nintendo) was not enough to save the format from a grim destiny so eminently foreseeable.

Atari Jaguar   1993

Reading this magazine six years ago, you'd be forgiven putting down a deposit for Atari's ambitious 64bit console. But this was a time when texture-mapped polys were rare elements, not the stock in trade of every Tom, Dick and Harry codeshop in existence. The lustre faded from the Jaguar in spectacularly rapid fashion; regardless of the value evident in the likes of *Cybermorph* and *Tempest 2000*, the hardware began to date almost by the week. Another Atari failure, then.

3DO   1993

Trip Hawkins' dream of creating a standard gaming platform, essentially the console equivalent of a stable PC environment, was laudable (and one that may still come into effect if Sony has its way), but his ambition exceeded the technology at his disposal. Despite being the first console to convincingly throw around large amounts of texture-mapped polygons, the excitement surrounding the 3DO rapidly dissolved once it became clear what Sony and Sega had planned for their 32bit consoles. It did not prevent a number of intriguing 3DO titles coming to fruition (two appear in **Edge**'s top 100), nor did it dampen Panasonic's spirits (the company produced a top-loading version of its R.E.A.L. Player to complement its original front-loading design), but the format sadly proved an ultimately fruitless exercise.

Amiga CD32   1993

Commodore really should have known better. Its first multimedia machine, the CD-TV, had died on its backside, while the technology with which it proposed to drive its push into the console realm (an Amiga 1200, to all intents and purposes) was already showing its age. But the company battled on – to eventual, predictable ruin.

Nintendo Virtual Boy   1995

How Nintendo gave the greenlight to this piece of hardware still now remains a mystery. Utilising hardware from Massachusetts-based Reflection Technology, the machine produced a red-saturated, convincing 3D display. The machine was hardly suited to extended periods of use, but then few gamers minded, since only a paltry number of VB titles were worth investing any time in. The late Gumpei Yokoi, who oversaw the machine's design and production, left Nintendo following the machine's abysmal reception at retail.

HANDHELDS/PORTABLES

If the hardware showcased over the last nine pages demonstrates innovation, consider another bunch at least as remarkable

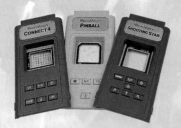

Microvision

1979

The first ever LCD cart-based console, the Microvision boasted cartridges like *Bowling* and *Pinball*, all controlled via an analogue paddle at the base of the machine. Despite over ten cartridges being released, none bettered the packed-in *Blockbuster*, which thanks to the oversensitive controller still offers an incredible level of challenge. Unusually, the European Microvision is far superior to the US original, with proper plastic keys, and chrome-style nameplates.

Coleco Total Control 4
1981

In 1981 Coleco took LED tabletop gaming to dizzy heights with the interchangeable TC4. While the four accompanying cartridges include new screen overlays, they do little to modify gameplay.

Entex Adventure Vision

1982

Entex released the unusual AdventureVision in 1982. Strangely, the machine uses a spinning mirror and red LEDs to create a 3D effect. The machine was famously unpopular and spawned only four cartridges, though a version of *Defender* did become available.

Epoch Game Pocket Computer
1984

Seen by many Otaku as the inspiration behind Nintendo's Game Boy, the chunky GPC fits neatly into the divide between the MB Microvision and Nintendo's machine. The 75x64-pixel screen is adequate enough to provide puzzle and simple action games, but a lack of consumer interest meant that, only four games were ever released for the unit.

Nintendo Game Boy

1988

The most successful videogame console of all time, Nintendo's portable wonder uses 8bit Z80 architecture that has been tweaked and refined since the first units hit an expectant Japanese audience along with what logically must be the most played game of all time, *Tetris*.

SuperVision
1989

While Quickshot's 1989 rival to the Game Boy should be ashamed of its mediocre range of games, a bizarre TV adaptor became available for the machine in the US, creating the first dual handheld and home console two-in-one.

PC Engine GT

1989

Arguably the most impractical handheld gaming device ever conceived, the PCEGT's most significant plus point was its complete compatibility with standard PC Engine titles. However, its high cost, and that fact that it required six batteries to get the unit up and running, meant that most users were of the extreme variety.

Donkey Kong Jr/Donkey Kong 3/Lion/ Rainshower/Mario Bombs Away   1981–91

The range of 60 Nintendo Game & Watch units ruled the world of LCD handheld gaming in a similar way to how the Game Boy does today. The first Game & Watch, *Ball*, was released in 1981, and despite initially slow sales the range continued until 1991 with the final widescreen game, *Mario the Juggler*.

Designed by Nintendo visionary Gumpei Yokoi, at their height double-screen machines like *Donkey Kong* and *Mario Bros* sold in their millions. During their lifespan the range was continually re-invented, including the introduction of innovative colour LCD tabletop and Panorama machines.

Amidar/Galaxian/Star Wars   various

Gakken's 1981 tabletop version of *Amidar* retains much of the playability of the arcade original. Coleco obtained official licences for the release of its range of arcade-like machines, and went on to

create undoubtedly the most accurate tabletop versions of all, including *Galaxian*. Licences have always driven portables, and with its 1978 *Star Wars*, Kenner typically skimped on gameplay.

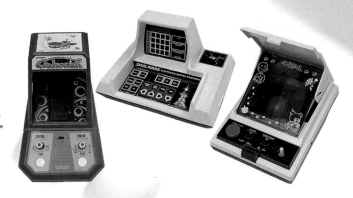

NEC PC Engine LT   1988

Released in Japan in 1988 for the equivalent of £600, the rarest of all PC Engine incarnations includes a

high-quality screen and built-in TV tuner. Truly the Rolls Royce of portable gaming systems, the LT is a fan's classic.

Atari Lynx   1990

Originally designed by software publisher Epyx under the codename Handy, the Lynx project was snaffled up by an Atari keen to break into the handheld market. The format played host to a number of

decent coin-op conversions and some fine original titles, but despite the machine's technical capacity, restrictive battery life and weak development support outside of the US finally signalled its death knell.

Sega Game Gear   1990

Essentially a cut-down Master System (an adaptor eventually made it possible to play MS games, to varying degrees of success, on the small screen), the Game Gear enjoyed a honeymoon period in the

UK thanks to the availability of *Sonic* and puzzle favourite *Columns*. In the face of Nintendo's super-durable Game Boy, however, the system's lifespan was always going to be limited.

Sega Nomad   1995

On the back of booming Genesis sales in the US, 1995 saw Sega release a long-awaited Genesis handheld. The Nomad's high-definition LCD screen and huge library of games couldn't outweigh the pain of the machine's high price, and stiff competition from

the Game Boy. Some may say the blatant Game Gear styling also did little to add kudos to the machine. To Sega's credit, though, it was even possible to play 32X titles on the machine, and Master System games were compatible via the official adaptor.

LARA

THE OFFICIAL LARA CROFT MAGAZINE

DESIGNED FOR LIFE

The inside story of Tomb Raider's sexy heroine!

TOMB RAIDER EXPOSED!
Lara's secret report • Exclusive pictures • The real lives of the Tomb Raider team!

THE LAST REVELATION
Latest news • Win a life-size Lara • How to get involved in the next Tomb Raider game • Meet the people who live for Lara!

ON SALE NOW!

TESTSCREEN

The definitive monthly assessment of the world's latest videogames

Dreamcast: the format that would be king (were it allowed)

If there's one type of reader correspondence that refuses to go away, it's the letter accusing **Edge** of having an anti-Sega agenda. To the freakish minds whose paranoia drives such allegations, the magazine you hold in your hands was singlehandedly responsible for the failure of the Saturn, is guilty of producing anti-Dreamcast propaganda, and even brought about the departure of Bernie Stolar from SOA (probably).

How could **Edge** possibly benefit by operating such policies? It could not. Which is why it does not.

However, Sega does seem intent on making its 128bit format hard to like. Requests for screenshots and product information from **Edge** and other specialist mags have not been met. Press discs haven't been sent out. System discs (which allow pre-master software to run on a DC) were slow to arrive. Modem-ready Euro DCs were delivered to the press three weeks after they were available in the high street. And, significantly, **Edge** has received a grand total of two phone calls from Sega Europe in the last eight months.

(To its credit, Powerhouse PR, the independent company hired by Sega to provide general press support, sends out whatever Sega makes available – usually game code – whenever it gets it.)

But if the specialist press has a rough time, spare a thought for lifestyle publications: some journalists are still waiting to receive Dreamcast system discs, which makes putting together game reviews rather difficult.

Consider how inept Sega looked when, less than two weeks before it was intending to go live in the UK, it announced a 21-day delay. Add to this the absolute mess the company has recently made with its Australian launch, and you'd be forgiven for thinking there was a mole at work within the walls of Sega HQ, engineering a maze of problems for the company.

And yet despite everything, **Edge**'s view of Dreamcast remains unaffected – as it rightly should. It is a great machine with some hugely promising software on the horizon. And healthy hardware sales have ensured a growth in development support, which is a positive sign for the machine's future.

But as with any format, substandard software will not be tolerated. And despite being a relatively new system, Sega's machine already has its share of shovelware. This happens to every console. But still the letters come, claiming that *Tokyo Highway Battle* is on a par with *Gran Turismo*. Please, Sega paranoiacs, do yourselves a favour – cut out the middle man: throw your letters straight into the bin the moment you've written them. Thanks.

Sonic Adventure, Power Stone and **Soul Calibur** are out there and showing what Dreamcast can do, flying in the face of Sega's apparent efforts to make progress difficult for the capable 128bit format

Index

Every issue, **Edge** evaluates the best, most interesting, hyped, innovative or promising games on a scale of ten, where five naturally represents the middle value. A game receiving a 'seven out of ten', for example, is a very competent title with noticeable flaws but which should still appeal to a considerable range of players. It does, after all, score two points above average and should therefore not be considered as such.

Edge's rating system is fair, progressive and balanced. An average game deserves an average mark – not, as many believe, seven out of ten.

Videogames on the **Edge**

Some of the crustier picks from Edge's 100, all serving to stir up the office

Secret of Mana (SNES) SquareSoft
Simultaneous threeplayer action-RPGs are hardly ten a penny, but when the defining example is of this quality, that's not a problem. Sublime stuff.

The Need for Speed (3DO) EA
The original and still the best, the rock-solid 3DO version of EA's ongoing series offers playability none of its successors has ever managed to match.

Shinobi (Coin-op) Sega
It popped out of nowhere in 1987, but this *Rolling Thunder* in ninja garb hastily attracted lovers of action gaming at its most polished. Scarily addictive.

Rampart (Coin-op) Atari
Another simultaneous threeplayer title to warm **Edge** Towers this month, this forgotten Atari classic divides loyalties among friends like few others.

HALF-LIFE: OPPOSING FORCE

A pitched exchange of ammunition over a broken bridge, a death-defying, two-rope swing over a chasm... *Opposing Force* offers a wealth of set-pieces

The Black Ops personnel, the bane of Freeman in *Half-Life*, turn on their military peers in *Opposing Force* for fantastic cat-and-mouse battles

While *Opposing Force*'s additions to the *Half-Life* cast of monsters are not outstanding, this creature (above) is fast and thoroughly alarming at close quarters

There is a series of unspoken laws that mission packs for firstperson shoot 'em ups adhere to. It's fair to anticipate a few new weapons, to expect a couple of inferior assailants to make their unspectacular debut, and for familiar textures to be punctuated by fresh art. Less videogame creation, more preaching to the converted, the add-on pack is forever a satisfying but pale reflection of its inspiration. Or is it?

Entwining its story with that of *Half-Life*, *Opposing Force* makes many casual references to its host title. Casting the player as one of the troops sent in to deal with the Black Mesa debacle, occasional familiar sights and references to scientist superhero Gordon Freeman lend it an air of credibility that many mission packs lack.

Its tempo and progression are reminiscent of Valve's tale, too, offering little more than standard FPS fare at times – and then, suddenly, so much more. It's an acute yet seemingly elementary gameplay aspect so many firstperson shooters continuously fail to incorporate.

Although its handful of new monsters are far from inspiring, the manner in which they are introduced is thoroughly atmospheric. In many respects, they typify *Opposing Force* in a curiously adroit manner. Taking the form of a narrative set-piece, these first encounters are almost entirely aural and allusive, rivalling comparable *Half-Life* moments. However, later you get to fight these creatures in an anticlimactic exchange of projectiles, and ten minutes on, they become just another alien genus appearing in predictable packs.

Predictably, there are new weapons to play with. Chief among these is a high-powered machine gun which propels your character

backwards when fired. Yet the most ambitious, perhaps, is a gun based on ceilings, hugging barnacles. Although it inflicts no damage it can be used to bridge gaps by attaching its telescopic tongue to any piece of organic matter. Sadly, unlike the grappling hooks that so enrich multiplayer *Quake II*, it is only of use when *Opposing Force*'s designers have supplied the requisite scenery, generally when they wish the device to be a solution to a problem.

Likewise, the much-publicised ability to climb and swing on ropes is used sparingly. Given the basic nature of the physics which govern their movement, this is unsurprising. And it's hardly the most engaging activity.

Visually, *Opposing Force* is no

Format: **PC**

Publisher: **Havas**

Developer: **Gearbox**

Price: **£30**

Release: **Out now**

With its atmospheric lighting, the *Half-Life* engine (borrowed from id and tweaked to pieces in parts) is perfect for rendering situations such as those shown here. But stuck in an enclosed space with a seemingly invulnerable alien, death is inevitable

less evocative than its parent title. Its set-pieces are just as well choreographed and despite an obvious over use of *Half-Life* textures, its locations are distinct. New character models, including a rotund Barney and a selection of soldiers with excellent facial animation, are also noteworthy.

But once again this aesthetic competence is outperformed in many respects by a sensory peer: its use of sound is, like *Half-Life,* outstanding.

The night-vision goggles replace *Half-Life*'s atmospheric torch

There is a surfeit of independent *Half-Life* add-ons on the **Internet.** *Opposing Force* **distinguishes itself by offering a markedly more professional,** polished experience

It must be said that there is a surfeit of indepedent *Half-Life* level add-ons on the Internet, but *Opposing Force* distinguishes itself by offering a markedly more professional, polished experience.

At times, however, it suggests greater depth and more features than it actually possesses. Like *Half-Life,* supporting characters are introduced at regular intervals. Better still, it poses elementary puzzles to solve by using these human resources effectively, such as escorting an engineer to a locked door, or a medic to a wounded soldier. But then, abruptly, your character is alone once more, compelled

by a trick of geography to leave companions behind.

In aspiring to match *Half-Life*'s remarkable standards, *Opposing Force* is a more engrossing adventure than its many elementary, moribund peers.

Of course, Valve did it first and, to be brutally frank, did it better. But developer Gearbox should not be disheartened. Even as a piggyback product its work rivals a number of standalone titles. It promises more than it ultimately delivers, but, as a child of *Half-Life,* it also delivers far more than most.

Edge rating:

Seven out of ten

Knowing how best to use human assets is the key to solving certain puzzles. This, however, is an under-exploited feature. Perhaps one for *Half-Life 2*?

MEDAL OF HONOR

Many of the characters animations are best demonstrated by the athletic ways in which the enemy soldiers die. (Above) The effect of a bazooka

(Top) Going undercover requires the use of pass papers not a gun. (Above) Each sub-level objective is completed by placing bombs as shown by the red box

One of the most tense and claustrophobic missions in *Medal of Honor* is fighting through dark, enemy-infested woods to infiltrate a fortress

In a year which has seen *Quake II* and *Rainbow Six* make the journey to PlayStation, it's refreshing to play an original shooter that pushes Sony's hardware to its limits. And in such surprising ways.

Wipeout 3 used hi-res textures and *Dino Crisis* offered polygonal backgrounds – but *Medal of Honor*'s AI and character animation rank with the best of any game, on any hardware.

It's a remarkable achievement, particularly when compared to some of DreamWorks' previous titles, such as *Trespasser* and *T'ai Fu*.

The developer has obviously spent a lot of time worshipping at the altar of *GoldenEye*. *Medal of Honor* has a similar aiming system, mission structure and pace.

You can't just burst into a room full of enemies and expect to walk away. And while it doesn't have the finesse of Rare's masterpiece, it's far more playable than the current clutch of firstperson shooters.

Set in the period around D-Day, June 1944, the game follows the progress of Lieutenant James Patterson, a member of the American special force organisation, the Office of Strategic Services.

There are seven missions, offering varied and authentic locations and armaments. Captain Dale Dye, Spielberg's consultant for 'Saving Private Ryan,' was also the game's historical adviser.

These missions range from destroying a giant railgun to rescuing European art treasures and recovering papers from a captured intelligence officer. Each one is split into multiple sections, creating 24 levels with their own objectives. These are relatively simplistic and involve little more than planting explosives on various pieces of military equipment.

But where *Medal of Honor* really impresses is its overall atmosphere. Even in the opening moments of the game when you are moving along French country lanes, enemies seem to pop out of nowhere. There's an undeniable sense of danger.

Some of the best touches are the undercover missions in which Patterson dons a German uniform. Players must carefully take out German officers with silenced weapons in order to steal their passes. It is then possible to fulfil the objectives undetected.

Later levels are more visceral and dominated by **powerful machine gun nests and snipers** that must be carefully located before they can be eliminated. **Caution is crucial and the tension palpable**

Format: **PlayStation**

Publisher: **EA**

Developer: **DreamWorks**

Price: **£30**

Release: **Out now**

There are only 12 different weapons in *Medal of Honor* but they are all authentically modelled. (Above) The Remington combat shotgun proves effective when used against vicious guard dogs in the sewers underneath a French town. Other weapons include the tommy-gun, hand grenades and a sniper rifle

Later levels are more visceral and dominated by powerful machine gun nests and snipers which must be carefully located before they can be eliminated. Caution is crucial and the tension palpable.

The sweeping musical score, recorded with Seattle Symphony Orchestra, is powerful and the roar of guns provides necessary gravitas.

There are hundreds of lines of well used dialogue, too. In one level, the

Germans even use a loudspeaker to warn the American spy he is surrounded and should give up.

The game's only failing is the usual one seen in US games. Health packs and ammo are generously supplied and levels can be successfully finished despite heavy damage.

Technically, DreamWorks has really pushed PlayStation's capabilities. Character animation is fantastic. Soldiers lean around corners, firing their guns with one hand. They clutch their wounds when hit by a bullet or are blown backwards if caught by a shotgun or grenade blast. Some even die with their finger on the trigger, their guns firing randomly as they enter death throes.

The AI is equally impressive, with soldiers running to set off alarms and alert their comrades, diving and rolling into cover when fired at, getting reinforcements and even throwing or

kicking grenades back towards you. Only its relative brevity and ease let *Medal of Honor* down. DreamWorks seems to have significantly toned down the AI's toughness during its testing phase, compared with the previous version that **Edge** grappled with.

Another quibble is the two player deathmatch which is solid rather than exciting. There are only seven different arena and five sets of weapons – it's certainly no *GoldenEye*-killer.

But these are small fry compared with the overall experience. Like *Hidden & Dangerous* on the PC, *Medal of Honor* is a refreshing reminder that good, original games can still come out of nowhere. It may not have a big movie licence attached but non-N64 owners have a new game in their sights.

Edge rating:

Eight out of ten

The two player mode is solid but *Medal of Honor* is all about a great oneplayer experience

The required snow level is set in Austria, where you have to stop the Germans blowing up Europe's art treasures

ZOMBIE REVENGE

Though the game has only seven levels, most of them are generously lengthy. As *Zombie Revenge* occurs within the timescale of *The House of the Dead*, one of the levels takes place in and around the *HOTD* coin-op's setting (right)

Z *ombie Revenge* made its original appearance on the monitors of Naomi-powered coin-ops back in 1998 as a side story to *The House of the Dead* series (set around the timeframe of *THOTD*).

Unsurprisingly, this is as faithful a conversion as DC *The House of the Dead 2* was, which means there's little to tell coin-op and console versions apart in visual terms. Both feature reasonably animated zombie killers blowing the limbs off the impressively detailed undead, against complex, solid-looking backdrops.

Admittedly, some of the boss characters you encounter throughout the game's seven extensive levels are oddly angular in appearance, but

these are rare occurrences. Generally speaking, there are more than enough polys to go around. Visually, this is an accomplished title, then.

In terms of gameplay, little has changed from the coin-op original, either. After choosing one of three zombie slayers, one or two players must shoot, punch and kick their way through to meet the inevitable baddest of bad guys.

The three-dimensional environments allow a fair amount of freedom, and you must progress to each new section within an allocated time period.

Throughout the game, many weapons lie around waiting to be picked up. There are dual handguns,

shotguns, machine guns, flame throwers, chain guns, grenades, remote mines, laser guns, pipes, axes, and even an insanely satisfying power drill.

As you negotiate the levels, your character automatically locks on to the nearest zombie, and the longer you wait before firing, the higher the amount of damage you'll cause (the colour scheme of the target changes from green to red).

Should you run out of ammo (or if you're looking for a more personal involvement with your undead foes), you can always resort to hand-to-hand combat. Simple yet effective combinations including throws can be unleashed with a few rapid button presses. It's an effective alternative. Get bitten by a zombie, though, and in typical B-movie style you become infected – it's then a good idea to pick up one of the

There are dual handguns, shotguns, machine guns, flame throwers, chain **guns, grenades,** remote mines, **laser guns, pipes, axes, and** even an insanely satisfying **power drill**

Level four's sequence requires stopping a train while fending off zombies. Sadly, there are no other sections as 'complex'

Format: **Dreamcast**

Publisher: **Sega**

Developer: **In-house**

Price: **¥5,800 (£35)**

Release: **Out now (Japan)**

March (UK)

The bosses are a varied bunch and reasonably accomplished. They're not the toughest, though, so tweaking the difficulty level is an option

In true Sega coin-op form, the voice acting in cut-scenes is awful (top). Two of the home version's extra games: Fighting (centre) and VS Boss Mode (above)

antidotes that are more than likely to be dropped by your lifeless adversaries.

Resist the temptation to switch the game to 'free play' mode and *Zombie Revenge* should provide you with a significant challenge, though hardly a diverse one. Other than having to pull a lever to stop the runaway train on which you are travelling before the time runs out (while simultaneously fighting off the armies of the undead in level four), it's a very standard, linear affair.

This is a regrettable residual effect stemming from the game's arcade parentage, and Sega has acknowledged this by including a number of home improvement options, although they ultimately fail in their bid to prolong the game's lifespan.

Initially, the most appealing of the four is probably Fighting Mode, which pits two players against each other in an attempt at a one-on-one beat 'em

up option. Sadly, matches last little more than 15 seconds; the first player to pick up a weapon more often than not ends up as the last one standing.

Gun Mode, meanwhile, sees one player go through the game with massively overpowered weaponry, whereas Bare Knuckle Mode sees hand-to-hand combat becoming more effective, and

ammo levels reduced accordingly.

Finally, VS Boss Mode (as in *THOTD2*) allows individual confrontations with the game's end-of-level bosses played against a timer.

Of more interest, though not necessarily any more playable, are the four VMU modes you can download, including the necessarily simplistic *Zombie Fishing* and *Zombie Doubt*, although their existence hardly constitutes purchasing a VMU unit.

Ultimately, *Zombie Revenge* is a repetitive experience. But if you regularly play videogames in the company of a friend, and are prepared to pace your progress and learn some of the characters' more intricate moves, it's still capable of providing a taste of plain and simple, arcade-faithful entertainment.

Edge rating:

Five out of ten

To its credit, *Zombie Revenge* offers a comprehensive array of weaponry, but they are not all as ludicrous (or as satisfying) as the power drill (left)

CHU-CHU ROCKET

Format: **Dreamcast**

Publisher: **Sega**

Developer: **In-house**

(Sonic Team)

Price: **¥5,800 (£35)**

Release: **Out now (Japan),**

March (UK)

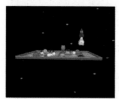

The game's only real noticeable move into 3D land occurs at the end of the level (once time runs out) when the camera decides to pan around the playing area

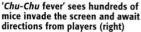

'*Chu-Chu* fever' sees hundreds of mice invade the screen and await directions from players (right)

E ffortlessly the most refreshing title to arrive at **Edge**'s office this year, *Chu-Chu Rocket* presents its case by offering up one of the best multiplayer experiences coupled with Sonic Team's usual attention to gameplay and a balance missing from other titles.

The concept is brain-achingly simple – guide as many mice into your rocket as you can within the time allocation. Whoever has the largest amount of mice when the counter reaches zero wins.

The control system is even simpler: move your colour-coded cursor around the board using either the D-pad or the analogue stick. Lay down directional instructions (up to three at a time) for the mice to follow by pressing one of the four buttons.

Their position on the joypad corresponds to the direction you wish the mice to take. This means that X is

left, B is right, Y up and A down. And that's it, you're ready to go.

There are other elements to contend with, of course. Cats wander around the board eating up mice with an insatiable appetite, and should a feline step aboard your rocket then the number of mice it consumes is immediately taken off your total.

There are bonus mice, naturally. These offer players the chance to radically redress the balance of total mice captured by instigating a series of random events.

Oneplayer mode offers a series of puzzle-based boards for you to clear (some of them fiendishly tricky) or the opportunity to play the main game against CPU opponents (whose AI level is selectable).

But absolutely nothing compares with the thrill of competing against human opponents. Either in teamplay (two on two) or in a fourplayer free-

for-all, *Chu-Chu Rocket* is utterly addictive. It's also one of the most frantic videogaming episodes you're ever likely to engage in; not only is the pace relentless but the game itself will quickly degenerate into a treacherous environment in which your opponents will sabotage your carefully planned route, stealing your mice and sending a cat your way instead.

Everything hangs in the balance until the very end – whether you're leading or trailing by literally hundreds of mice there's no guarantee that your fortunes will not have U-turned by the time the whistle blows.

Grab three friends, buy three joypads and load *Chu-Chu Rocket*. This is videogaming excellence in its purest form.

Edge rating:

Eight out of ten

Get one of the pink mice to board your rocket and a bonus event is randomly selected (left). Puzzle stages require a logical approach (right)

FIGHTING FORCE 2

Format: **DC (version tested)/PlayStation**

Publisher: **Eidos**

Developer: **Core Design**

Price: **£40**

Release: **Out now**

(Above) The environments maybe dull but _Fighting Force 2_'s end-of-level bosses are bizarre. (Right) Even zombies make an appearance

Character animations are suited to a beat 'em up, and there is a variety of blunt objects to use

D espite the success of _Fighting Force_, it always received a lukewarm critical response. At least Core knew it had the advantage of a sequel to refine the concept. Gone are the confusing multiple characters and the thankless punch-kick combinations of the original. This time, the game revolves around only one character, Hawk Manson, while the beat 'em up action has been upgraded with an arsenal of weapons. The incentive is now to bang-bang, punch and kick.

And the basic structure of the game is a great improvement. Control is good with strafe, jump, side rolls and a firstperson mode included. There's even 180-degree rotation. The inventory system is well thought out as well.

Each weapon type from handgun to knife, grenade and two-handed weapon has a specific location on Hawk's bod – as the shotgun is selected, he will reach and pull it off his back. This means Hawk can only carry up to five weapons, opening strategic quandaries about which weapons should be carried.

Unfortunately, for all this, _Fighting Force 2_ is ultimately a dull game.

There is a void where gameplay should exist. Across the nine levels, the only activity is to go into a room, destroy everything, collect the keys and any items and then open the next door and repeat, _ad nauseam_, until you reach the badly balanced end-of-level bosses.

The lack of consistency in the level design doesn't help much either. In fact, sometimes it feels like playing a 'what's what of videogaming.' The jungle base bizarrely ends up with the skeletons from _Tomb Raider IV_ and the chemical plant is overrun by _Resident Evil_-type zombies, while _GoldenEye_'s automatic miniguns appear in the last two levels.

There also seems to be a fundamental misbalance between the weapon and the beat 'em up aspects.

There are so many guns stashed in the environments that there's no need to move in for hand-to-hand combat, and that's the only time there's any drama in the game.

Other bugbears, such as over-sensitive falling damage, stupid AI and doors that can't be reopened once passed through, make an appearance as well. The result is a wasted opportunity. The signs were good, the foundations solid and Dreamcast's sparkling graphics and capable sound qualities are put to good use. But it feels as if _Fighting Force 2_ has been rushed out for Christmas. No polish. Little enjoyment. Who's going to wait for the next instalment?

Edge rating:

Four out of ten

The reliance on guns in _Fighting Force 2_ is shown by its firstperson mode. They become more important in later levels to the detriment of hand-to-hand combat

INTERNATIONAL TRACK & FIELD 2

Format: **PlayStation**

Publisher: **Konami**

Developer: **In-house**

Price: **£40**

Release: **January**

IT&F2 introduces seven new events (in five new categories) but of all these only the men's weightlifting (main) is the closest to the original's gameplay ethics. Some of the updated events such as pole vault (above, left) have been over complicated

For the women's diving (top) and gymnastics vault events, you must first select the move you wish to perform. The kayak race will test your concentration

Konami has done a *Nagano*. That is, it has taken a perfectly playable title (based on the 1997 Winter Olympics and one of **Edge**'s favourite mulitplayer ventures – see Top 100 games, p52) and laboured over the clean, simple controls to the point where it interferes with play.

There are improvements. There's Dual Shock support and graphically things look suitably advanced, with polygonally-modelled athletes moving about while some of the events are played out against a pleasant dusk or late evening setting.

There's better presentation, too, both ingame (such as an overhead shot showing the position of your competitor's foot on the ground during a long jump) and throughout the various menus, which also notify you of the controls for the next event.

And, of course, there are new events. In addition to weightlifting, there's women's springboard diving, two cycling contests (sprint and 1km time trial), a 500-metre kayak race and a women's gymnastics vault.

A 50-metre women's freestyle swimming competition replaces the 100-metre race found in the original *Track & Field* PlayStation title. To these you can add the men's 100-metre sprint, long jump, pole vault, hammer throw and javelin, which are also from the title's predecessor.

The discus, high jump, triple jump, shot put and 110-metre hurdle events are no longer featured. The problem is, that of all the new events, only weightlifting remains true to the essence of the arcade original.

Yes, the cycling events offer the traditional button-bashing approach, but somehow they prove less engaging than the other events on offer (the 1Km time trial, in particular, takes the concept a touch too far,

and requires the player to maintain a gruelling pace on the controls for 60-odd seconds).

Elsewhere, the diving lacks a crucial dose of fluidity, pole vault is over-complicated, and swimming is drastically slowed down, which is more realistic but far less satisfying. Conversely, javelin is better, and kayak racing, while it possibly would have benefited from a little more vitality, is a good test of nerves. In fact, it requires surprising levels of concentration.

All in all, *International Track & Field* isn't a bad game – with four players and a multitap it's a very enjoyable and competitive affair – but ultimately, given the playability evident in its predecessor, you can't help but end up expecting a little more than what's on offer.

Edge rating:

Six out of ten

ISS PRO EVOLUTION

It's hard to suitably communicate just how well-observed *ISSPE*'s brand of football truly is. The sheer depth of its tactical awareness and its outstanding realism make it almost more revolution than evolution

Format: **PlayStation**

Publisher: **Konami**

Developer: **KCET**

Price: **£40**

Release: **January**

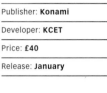

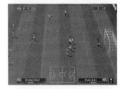

At first, *Evolution*'s strategy pages are daunting – and perhaps rightly so. It allows almost pinpoint manipulation of any given formation

As a representation of its real-life inspiration, *ISS Pro Evolution* is virtually peerless. It is, without question, the most well observed, tactically astute football game of the millennium. Consistently playable and challenging as a oneplayer experience, its multiplayer credentials are equally comprehensive.

Matches in *Evolution* are dynamic, multi-faceted events, and it has a depth that makes its contemporaries appear shockingly lightweight. Each player has a huge catalogue of characteristics to reflect that individual's area of expertise. Tony Adams, for example – referred to as Adamms, due to the lack of an appropriate licence – is tall, heavy, and adept at telling challenges.

Michael Owen's misspelt alter ego, however, is diminutive and fleet of foot. In many other soccer games, the disparity in pace alone would render the Adamms of the virtual pitch impotent. *ISS Pro Evolution*, by way of exquisite AI routines and careful balancing, ensures that every strength has a natural foil of some description.

With the ball at the feet of a player under your control, it's hard not to marvel at the intelligent movement of your team-mates. Wing-backs make overlapping runs and attacking midfielders drop back to provide passing options. Granted, it is possible to charge through entire teams on the 'Easy' setting, but higher skill levels soon curtail this behaviour.

Refreshingly, *Evolution* empowers players with strategic flexibility. If you wish to hoof the ball over the top, or opt for elaborate passing *à la* Evansera Liverpool, it's your prerogative – and the game will evolve and adapt.

Sometimes, a match can degenerate into a free-for-all, with misplaced passes allowing end-to-end mayhem. It's immensely gratifying, in this instance, to put a foot on the ball – so to speak – and slow the game down to a manageable pace. Of course, such intricate, authentic football does not come without an attendant cost. At times, your team can run 'on rails' to a noticeable degree – although CPU assistance is fairly transparent.

Furthermore, it is not the most immediate of football games. But after just one week, few players would consider returning to the increasingly dismal *FIFA*, or its chasing pack of aspirant never-beens. What *Evolution* lacks, then, is a heavyweight licence; a through-ball into consumer consciousness. Without one, it will no doubt retain its role as a commercial runner-up. But, to paraphrase Keegan, **Edge** would just love it, just *love* it, if…

Edge rating:

Nine out of ten

THRASHER: SKATE & DESTROY

Format: **PlayStation**

Publisher: **Rockstar Games**

Developer: **Z-Axis**

Price: **£40**

Release: **January**

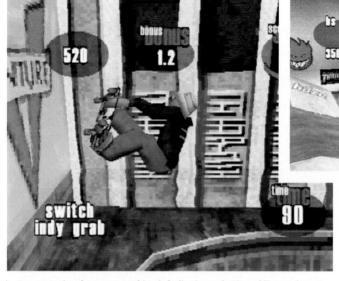

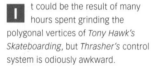
Accompanying the on-screen big-air frolics is a selection of licensed music tracks including the likes of 'Rapper's Delight' and 'Talkin' All That Jazz'

Expect to bail far more often than in other skating titles (above). *Thrasher* **demands a more technical and cautious approach to the urban pastime**

It could be the result of many hours spent grinding the polygonal vertices of *Tony Hawk's Skateboarding*, but *Thrasher's* control system is odiously awkward.

Or maybe it's just an indication that of the two games, *Tony Hawk's* developer Neversoft found the better solution (though, it has to be said, not the perfect one). Because here, controlling the skaters is overly convoluted. While a lot of practice makes it less so, it certainly isn't as intuitive or as fluid as it might be.

Neversoft also managed to prise better skater animation out of the PlayStation. While all the moves in *Thrasher* look like the real thing, there's a sluggishness to the action – as if things are not quite moving at the right speed – which, given the immediacy of acrobatic displays in Neversoft's game, can easily lead to frustration.

Furthermore, although it could be argued that there's a certain grittiness to *Thrasher's* environments that lend it extra authenticity (something Take Two has obviously striven for), the overall visual impact is less than that of *Hawk's*.

So *Thrasher* trails Neversoft's game in a number of key areas. But it certainly has some strengths of its own, too. For starters, there is a wider trick repertoire on offer (extra moves are made available by playing through levels, each requiring you to reach a particular score before further access can be made), and while the control system does take a while to get comfortable with, it is a more technical and less forgiving game than *Tony Hawk's*, which ups the challenge level considerably.

As a more realistic game, you won't find your skater surging high into the air when taking off a ramp in *Thrasher*. And because there's less height on jumps, you're far less likely to land 900s on a regular basis. Things are literally a lot more down to earth.

Also more authentic is the way you earn sponsorship throughout the game and get the opportunity to select different skatewear. This doesn't affect gameplay, but it's a touch which is likely to go down well with the skateboarding intelligentsia.

Those prepared to break through the barrier set up by the control method will be rewarded with a skateboarding game that, while not in the *Tony Hawk's Skateboarding* playability league, offers a sufficiently competent gameplay/identity mix to recommend it to those so enamoured with the pastime that they simply must experience every available videogame interpretation. E

Edge rating:

Six out of ten

Thrasher's **level structure is a tad less adventurous than current genre-leader** *Tony Hawk's Skateboarding*, **with fewer 'secret' areas to explore**

TOMORROW NEVER DIES

Of the activities on offer, the car sequence (top) probably hides its limitations best. Bosses must be shot 100 times (top right). *Horace Goes Skiing* offers more playability than *TND*'s piste action (right)

Format: **PlayStation**

Publisher: **Electronic Arts**

Developer: **Black Ops**

Price: **£40**

Release: **Out now**

Street lamp flare is new (top), thermal vision isn't (centre) and collision detection is in a league of its own(above): think you can get through that gap? Think again

Tomorrow Never Dies is one of those rare games that actually gets worse the more it is played.

It's not difficult to see why it is being released alongside new Bond film 'The World Is Not Enough' or why it is being backed by a monumental £2m marketing campaign, which is allegedly the biggest yet for a videogame.

TND is likely to need all the hype it can get to persuade gamers to pick up a copy.

Inevitably (and sadly) the strength of the licence alone will shift many units, possibly to people who see this as some kind of *GoldenEye* substitute for the PlayStation.

Hopefully, though, word of mouth will prevent many more from having the appalling misfortune of unwrapping this while sat around the Christmas tree.

The level select screen is taken straight from *GoldenEye*, as are some of the mission elements and structures. The control system is shocking, the 3D camera frightfully erratic, the enemy AI risible and the collision detection outrageous.

The motion capture is low grade, the cut scenes are unconvincing (and can't be skipped, even if you're replaying the level), the voice acting is uninspired and enemies magically regenerate (usually behind you, just to add to the frustration).

Not only is the graphical quality of the desperately barren environments poor, but there are record-breaking levels of polygon break up and the draw distance (particularly during the skiing sequences) leaves more than a little to be desired.

The significant consequences of all the above is that you're left with a title which offers little in terms of fluidity of play and there appear to be no discernable gameplay rewards.

There's no subtlety to *TND*'s contents, no finesse to anything it does. At one point, for instance, after being left in an interrogation room with nothing but a pair of cufflinks in Bond's inventory, the developer still feels the need to drop a hint that the player should use a gadget when close to the two-way mirror. No ordinary cufflinks? *Quelle surprise.*

In its defence, the sound effects are good (if not always in synch with the relevant onscreen action) and the overall presentation is reasonably accomplished. And with several modes of play, it offers plenty of variety.

Ultimately, *Tomorrow Never Dies* has the appearance of your least favourite first-generation PlayStation game. It doesn't, however, have the balls to play like one.

Edge rating:

Two out of ten

INDIANA JONES & THE INFERNAL MACHINE

Format: **PC**

Publisher: **Activision**

Developer: **LucasArts**

Price: **£30**

Release: **Out now**

Its engine may not provide a spectacular level of detail at close quarters, but *Infernal Machine* conveys a sense of scale with admirable aplomb

Combat, for so long the weakest element of Lara Croft's escapades, is a real problem within *The Infernal Machine*. But at least LucasArts gets the rope swinging right

Adequate cut-scenes punctuate play at set junctures

Entertainment software as a means of instant gratification? Those were the days. As 3D engines consolidate their position as the *de facto* medium for gaming experiences, learning curves continue to rise.

And the depth and sheer sense of involvement many developers seek to engender rarely lends itself to two or three-button interfaces. With few programmers external to the likes of Nintendo and Konami truly comprehending the worth of intuitive context sensitivity, awkward control systems, amateur camera work and bewildering button combinations are par for the course.

Indiana Jones & The Infernal Machine must be, then, a positively hateful game. You can almost feel its

potential. Its engine is geared towards distance and scale, its vistas artfully insinuate sweeping magnitude. Its premise, though highly derivative and almost ironic, is equally worthy. Indiana Jones in a *Tomb Raider*-style adventure? Wonderful.

But any enthusiasm is tempered during early levels. It is, in short, blighted by an awkward, poor designed control system. From jumps to the simple act of walking through corridors, even experienced gamers will find their patience tested.

Indy has a habit of moonwalking when caught against scenery and many of his (fairly disappointing) animation sequences are uncomfortably laboured.

It would be unfair to level the accusation of 'counter intuitive' but many will voice that suspicion.

Learn to live with its protagonist's inadequacies though, and *The Infernal Machine* becomes surprisingly compulsive. Unusually for LucasArts, its storyline and voice acting will leave many feeling fairly indifferent, yet its puzzle content is excellent.

Faced with a particular dilemma, it is enormously satisfying to craft an appropriate solution – and many of its

puzzles are pleasantly challenging. As time and experience reduce the control-oriented inadequacies to a medium-grade irritant, negotiating platforms actually becomes enjoyable.

Post-*Tomb Raider*, and with *Metal Gear Solid* and *Zelda* having set new standards for 3D control, *The Infernal Machine* presents an awkward dichotomy. Its basic play mechanics may be dated and lack subtlety, but the level design – first forays aside – is of a high standard. This conflict is one that many mainstream gamers will certainly be frustrated with.

Alongside the traditional learning curve, *The Infernal Machine* also has an acceptance curve – the period of time it takes for a player to become accustomed to its shortcomings.

The rating, then, reflects its worth to players who have the patience to brave its inadequacies. Fair-weather gamers beware.

Edge rating:

Six out of ten

Typically, Indy gets to use the occasional vehicle. These offer a welcome diversion, but are little more than that. And yes, there is a mine-cart ride

edge moves

Datascope
GAMES PEOPLE

ARE YOU GEARED UP FOR THE NEXT CENTURY?
WE ARE!

At the dawn of a new age, has there ever been a more appropriate time to break with the past? If you want to know where the best millennium opportunities are right now, get interactive with us. Formed in 1989, Aardvark Swift is the longest established games agency in the UK with many well known companies now using our services exclusively. The bottom line is if we don't have your details on file, you simply can't be considered for these opportunities - many of which are only advertised via ourselves. Don't miss out!

Programmers

Internet Programmers Unbelievable opportunity for C++, Java developers with games and internet background or interest. Superb benefits include action outings, adventure trips, free tickets for the footie, celebration parties, training courses in exotic locations etc. Work hard, play hard ethic, plus one of the best working environments around and flexible hours.............. ....£40-50k + Stock Options (Central London)

PC/PlayStation Programmers Premier developer. Maths/physics skills for dynamics & graphics related work. Preferably one published title......................£Neg (Scotland)

C/C++ Programmers (x2) Small team environment. Action style product. 3D team players needed with good maths/physics. ....£25-30k + Bonuses (East Midlands)

AI Programmer New cutting edge technology company seek background in evolutionary AI/biology, fuzzy logic, route finding, flocking etc. Excellent opportunity to assist design and implement own comprehensive AI system. ....£30-32k + Royalties (London)

Color Gameboy Programmers Many requirements nationally and a few home based options.

Home Based Programmers (x6) Rapidly expanding developer with well established streetwise management team. PC PSX and Dreamcast conversion work. 3D skills essential ....£Neg

Senior Games Programmer 3D strategy game with unique control system. Game logic and AI responsibilities. Well funded new venture, several big name players already on board ....£35k + Bonuses (South London)

Freelance PC Programmer Direct X skills required to assist in completion of famous cartoon character product. In house or home based option ....To £40k + Completion Bonus

Dreamcast Programmers Many opportunities nation-wide. Some with opportunity to work at the very heart of the development community - Japan! ....£Excellent

PlayStation 2 Programmers Project and vacancy notifications now coming through thick and fast. Call now and acquire valuable 'next gen' skills.

PC Programmers (x2) Gothic adventure product. Small experienced team. Excellent prospects.................£30k (Kent)

C/C++ Programmers (x3) Newly opened office of well established Midlands based development house. Graduate calibre candidates sought for platformer. City location ....£Neg (South Yorkshire)

PlayStation Programmers (x2) Urgent requirement for action adventure myth and magic type product. Long established company (pre Amiga). **to £35k (West Midlands)**

PlayStation Contract Programmer Home based or in house Well established company ....£Neg 4-6 months

AI Programmer. Ambitious, exciting company with unique technology developing highly original titles. Applicants require an up to date knowledge of latest AI techniques and a strong academic background ....

..£Highly competitive + Profit Related Bonus (London)

PlayStation Programmer Action adventure/platformer. Immediate start ....£High plus generous 'golden handshake' (South East)

C/C++ Programmers (x2) Knowledge of physics and AI required for PC strategy product. Part of secure multinational empire. Small team environment, well managed and funded organisation ....£30k basic (London)

Programmer Progressive organisation with highly innovative product require high quality experienced programmer with C++, AI, Win32 and 3D. Neural Networks and Artificial Life Systems advantageous. Creative company with leading edge technology...£25-35k (London)

Artists

Maya/Alias Animators Sequel to best seller. Mo Cap knowledge beneficial. Large, secure and well respected organisation.....................£25-30k + Bonuses (London)

Texture Artist Dpaint or Photoshop skills urgently needed by prestigious developer. 16 colour experience essential ....£22-28k (South West)

3D Studio Artists (x4) Established studio. Racing/Rally product. Mainly modelling.. ....£16-28k + Bonuses (North West)

Character Animator Well known company. Create range of low poly humans and animals in Max/Character Studio............ ....£24-28k + Bonuses (West London)

Home Based Artists Rapidly expanding developer with high work load. Good experience with 3DS Max, Character Studio and Photoshop essential. (Not 2D Gameboy work)..........£Neg

3D Studio Max Artists New project. PC Strategy game. To commence Q1 2000 ....£Neg + Bonuses (South West)

3D Studio Max Artist (x2) Creative all rounders required for new, second project team. Share and develop ideas in an open relaxed environment. Award winning, influential products. Exclusive to ourselves.........................£20-32k (South East)

Lead Artist Games experience and 3D S Max essential for senior role on sports product. Central location. USA owned company. Exclusive...................£25-30k + Bonuses (London)

3DS Max Artists (x2) Developer utilising cutting edge engine technology require min 2 years experience and character creation for R/T action adventure product. Motivated team in non corporate environment ....£High + Bonuses + Royalty (London)

Animator Interactive adventure product for PC based on well known mystical character. Small team environment. 3D Studio Max preferred. Well established organisation ....to £24k + Bonus (Midlands)

Management

Studio Manager New vacancy. International developer. Established development studio. Big job big wage................... ....£70-90k (South East)

Executive Producer Internal and external responsibilities. Senior role working with some of the best known licences in the business ....£35-40k (North)

Producer Internal project manager required by hugely successful medium sized developer. Scheduling and tracking skills especially prized. Autonomous role.................................. ....c£35k (South East, not London)

Producers - anywhere and everywhere. Seems pretty much everybody's seeking good producers right now. Projects slipping possibly? - Surely not! (5 options in Midlands alone).

Creative Director State of the art new media studio. Experience of gaming web design and high end creative applications (eg Softimage) advantageous................................... ....c£40k + 30% Bonus + Car etc (North West)

Project Manager New vacancy at new studio. Head up and manage a small team of your own choice and create new game concepts ....£35-42k + Bonus + Benefits (Midlands)

External Producer Perform technical and gameplay advisory role for one of the industry's biggest names. Newly created vacancy ....£30k + Car + Bonuses

External Producer Famous name, highly successful and acquisitive company. Manage existing UK based portfolio of developers ....c£35k + Bonus (South)

Producers Position currently available at 3 separate organisations. All internal roles managing the development of quality products from initial design to final mastering to agreed costs and schedules. ....£24-38k Basic (Midlands)

Producer Good all rounder, preferably with technical bias sought for PSX2 futuristic blaster. Concept/design element in addition to scheduling. Big name company.............................. ....£35-38k + Bonuses (London)

Others

Sound Designers 3 vacancies. ....(South West, North East and Midlands)

Games Designers (x3) London based developer with strong product portfolio (no sports games) seek 3D graphics experience for cartoon style arcade/adventure and new racing title. Immediate start. ....£22-26k (South East)

Lead Testers High profile company. Experience of writing test plans needed. ....c£18k (West London)

Games Designer Two vacancies, one North and one South. Both require first rate knowledge of what makes a good game and excellent communication skills ....£25k + Bonuses

Overseas

Games Designer RTS product. Superb opportunity for a new start....£Neg + Visa (Australia) Senior Producer + Sound Designer, Senior Programmers, Art Director PlayStation/N64 development studio. 70 people. Big licence. Highly progressive company. Superb opportunities.......$Neg + Royalties + Stock Options and Health & other benefits. 3D Latest 3D technology. £Excellent (Sydney & Canberra) Programmer/Artists (USA) Well respected West Coast developer always in the market for "good Brits" to join team in sunny California. Company works for major publishers, are British owned and are just 7 miles from the beach.. ....$65-80k + Royalties, Medical and Legal Fees

Register by Sending a CV (& examples where applicable) to:
Aardvark Swift Consulting Ltd, Silicon House, Farfield Park, Wath upon Dearne, Rotherham, South Yorkshire S63 7DB
Tel: (01709) 876877   Fax: (01709) 760134   Email: SLD@ardswift.demon.co.uk
Many more vacancies at www.ardswift.co.uk

Please indicate locational preferences and salary guidelines. All enquiries and applications will be treated in the strictest confidence.

evolution
s t u d i o s

would like to wish

all our competitors

the very best of luck

in the new millennium.

You're going to need it.

The twilight days of the past millennium have proven to be a stellar time for Rare, with the release of Jet Force Gemini, Conker's Pocket Tales, Mickey's Racing Adventure and Donkey Kong 64 all in the space of a few frenetic months. But far from being spent, we're all fired up and thundering into 2000 armed with the forthcoming Perfect Dark, Banjo Tooie and a few secret bombshells to drop at the appropriate time . . .

Of course, there's always room for new blood in the team. So if you can offer us a focused talent, passion for your work and the dogged determination to see it through, get in touch.

Rare is currently recruiting the following :

GAME PROGRAMMERS

To code cutting edge software for current and future Nintendo hardware. Applicants must be fluent in C or Assembler. Enthusiasm for games a definite advantage.

3D ARTISTS

With imagination and a natural flair for creating detailed environments, characters or animation. Previous experience with 3D packages, particularly Maya, useful but not essential.

GAME BOY COLOUR ARTISTS

To join our dedicated Game Boy team in creating a variety of Nintendo handheld titles.

Please submit CVs and work examples to :

Personnel Dept.
Rare Ltd.
Manor Park
Twycross
Warwickshire
CV9 3QN

RAREWARE

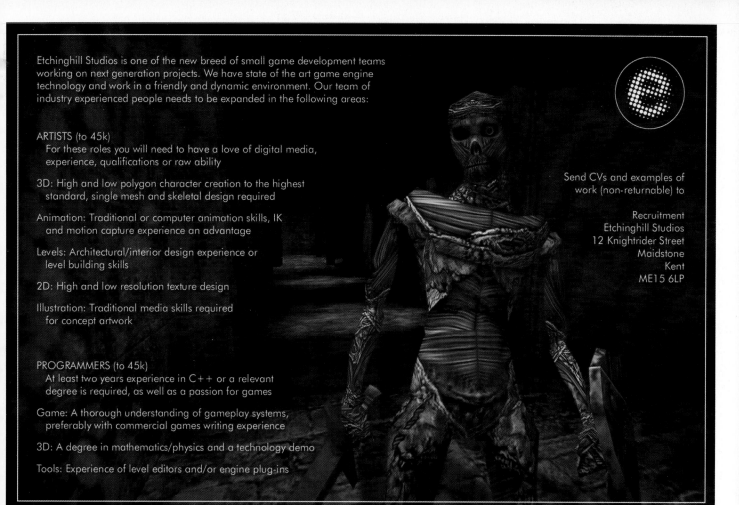

·RUNE·CRAFT·

Synopsis

As part of our continued expansion we are looking to recruit
additional talented individuals.
A well structured Company, incorporated in April 1997,
with a strong management infrastructure. Currently employing
65 in-house staff. The company has been able to attract
the right calibre of motivated, experienced staff through the work
ethic reflected in its employment policies.

Strengths we offer our staff:

- A great place to work from. Our newly refurbished, 6000 square

  foot, 3 storey, freehold studio is a very conducive environment.

- Excellent salaries.

- Paid overtime to all staff members - no bogus bonus schemes

- Loyalty inducing benefits such as a Company Pension Scheme

  and Private Medical Health Cover for all staff.

Artists

We are looking for talented individuals with all around skills to join our art department.

A prospective employee should be able to show good skills in both 2D and 3D art work, have a good understanding of the industry standard packages such as 3DS MAX and Photoshop and be comfortable with low polygon and low colour images.

Programmers

You must have strong 3D, maths and physics, C and C++, have worked in a senior programming level on at least 1 games title and enjoy working in a great environment.

To work on Dreamcast, PC, Playstation and Playstation 2.

·RUNE·CRAFT·

RuneCraft Limited,
The Old Eightlands Well,
Eightlands Road,
Dewsbury,
West Yorkshire

Contact : **WF13 2PF**

Tel: 01924 500817
Fax: 01924 500898

WWW.RuneCraft.co.uk
(Under Construction)

Research AND Development software engineers

DOLPHIN

ADVANCED GAMEBOY

ADVANCED **RENDERING** TECHNIQUES

SOFTBODY **SIMULATION**

PROCEDURAL **ANIMATION**

MATERIAL **SYNTHESIS**

REALTIME AUDIO COMPOSITION

Apply to:

Personnel Dept. Rare Ltd.

Manor Park, Twycross

Warwickshire CV9 3QN

Rage

DUE TO CONTINUED
GROWTH,
RAGE GAMES LTD
IS LOOKING TO RECRUIT

Location: Liverpool, Birmingham, Warrington, Newcastle and Sheffield.

We are looking for **CODERS, ARTISTS** and **DESIGNERS** keen to make a fast and rewarding move into a new millennium of games software.

Rage has recently seen the opening of two new studios in Warrington and Sheffield.

Rage Warrington presently comprises more than 30 of the brightest development professionals from the company formerly known as Digital Image Design Limited.

Rage Sheffield, also a hotbed of talent, presently houses 15 staff.

While continuing to build an enviable reputation for world-leading entertainment software on the PC, we are also busy working on the new generation of gaming consoles.

When it comes to ensuring the best in terms of work environment and remuneration, Rage has a reputation second to none. No hollow promises but a genuine share in success for individuals who make it happen.

Artists should know how to squeeze the best from 3D Studio Max and Photoshop. Coders should have experience in C or C++ with excellent maths or physics knowledge.

If you think we need to know about you, send your CV, stating studio preference, to: The Personnel Department, Rage Games Ltd., Martins Building, Water Street, Liverpool, L2 3SP Alternatively e-mail to: career.moves@war.rage.co.uk.

If possible, coders and artists are requested to include copies of work (not originals).

Creations

Crackers about Games?

To advertise in Edge *Moves*

call Emma Lewis or Neil Abraham

t: 020 7317 2628

e: emma.lewis@futurenet.co.uk
   neil.abraham@futurenet.co.uk

Free design service available

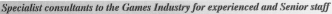

develop

videogame creation under the microscope

Meeting the guv'nors: Player Manager 2000 interfaces with the real thing

(Top) Paul Bracewell, of Fulham, keeps up to date with Elixir's _Revolution,_ while Coventry's Gordon Strachan can't believe that last refereeing decision

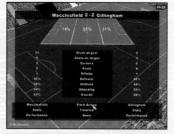

Watford and ex-England manager Graham Taylor attempts to get to grips with Anco's latest sim, _Player Manager 2000,_ in its friendly PlayStation incarnation

With the exception of David James' famous late-night/early-morning PlayStation habit, when it comes to computer games the closest most football stars seem to get is celebrity endorsement and hard cash in the bank.

Even in the more sedate world of football management games, it's the likes of George Graham, Arsene Wenger and Kevin Keegan who get their faces on the box, with little actual involvement in how the game plays.

But the final tweaking stage of Anco's latest game, _Player Manager 2000,_ witnesses a role reversal, with the game being tested for accuracy by some of the league's more down-to-earth managers. It should, hopefully, result in a more realistic experience, although the testing process has demonstrated the widely differing techniques used by real-life managers. Strangely, none of them admit to actually using a football management game – but they have seen their kids playing them. Watford's Graham Taylor confesses that he is still getting to grips with the technological revolution of the computer. He plans his team tactics with a box of Tiddlywinks and a Subbuteo pitch.

Fulham's Paul Bracewell has got straight to business, requesting the option for set team formations to be automatically applied throughout the game so he can set up an opening gambit for the first 15 minutes, then revert to a standard formation. At present, _Player Manager 2000_ allows you to change players' positions at any time, but does not allow preset formations.

Gordon Strachan, manager of Coventry, has proved himself to be skilled operator, too. Playing against Derby, his Coventry team went down to nine men but some canny restructuring saw them snatch a 1-0 victory: a feat that Anco's testers haven't managed. (Graham Taylor blamed a 5-0 drubbing at the hands of Man Utd on old player specs.)

Bracewell particularly enjoyed the three modes in which the actual game was displayed: ranging from simple topdown to an isometric side-on view. Fuelled by Al-Fayed's millions, Fulham want an eight-camera system at Craven Cottage, then the club can record all the players' game movements.

The transfer mode, meanwhile, provoked some wry smiles. Managers had to list what attributes they want and their price, then see who's available. "It's amazing that no players have come up [on the transfer list]," commented Bracewell, after his dream left-back failed to materialise for under £800,000.

"It's like real life. If you haven't got the budget, you can't get the top players." He eventually found someone for £600,000. And the outcome? One change that Anco will definitely be making, as proposed by both Strachan and Taylor, is the ability to see an opponent's formation superimposed on yours, so that relative strengths and weakness can be easily asserted.

"This is fantastic," reckoned Strachan. "I'm not going to tell my kids that, though – they'll want to play me."

WorkStation

A series of experiments appears to be inspiring the revolutionary creations at CyberLife Technology, as the company's **Lisa de Araujo** reveals to **Edge**. Staff at the developer responsible for artificial life sim _Creatures 3_ (which simulates the very processes and structures of life itself) clearly take their research very seriously indeed.

Skeleton "This poor developer topped himself after a particularly hard milestone. Unfortunately, it seems to be a common occurrence. We've been force-feeding the programmers to no avail!"

Sea Monkeys "Even though we create artificial life forms at CyberLife, we still support the undead realspace variety. Honestly, they are alive and there are five of them swimming even now! Presumably they're pining for the river just outside the window"

Dead Kenny "Finally, we have poor Kenny. We came up with a variety of amusing ways to kill Kenny and captured quite a few for our webcam. This was by far the best and we've since decided to preserve him for posterity"

Members of the development community (sane or otherwise) are invited to email WorkStation submissions to **edge@futurenet.co.uk**

After co-founding Lionhead Studios with Peter Molyneux, **Demis Hassabis** set up his own development house, Elixir Studios. In the latest instalment of his exclusive diary, he sets out to explain the individual roles of the team behind *Republic: The Revolution*

Bright ideas

You've got a game idea, so how do you set about turning it into a game? And more specifically, who are the people that make games and what do they do day to day? Over the next few months I'll be discussing the roles of the different members of Elixir and their role in making *Republic: The Revolution*, our first game [see **E**78].

Elixir has two main designers – myself and Joe McDonagh. The role of a good lead designer is manifold. It is up to you to provide the initial concept for the game. It's essential that you have a strong vision. You then need a

another can be a Scottie dog…"). To do this you need a good imagination and the ability to communicate your ideas to people.

The mechanical side is much harder and the least understood part of the job. It involves writing the rules to the game, which is a process of enumerating and calibrating key game mechanics. How powerful is a rocket launcher in relation to an axe? How much money should a player pay if he lands on Park Lane with two houses and, crucially, are these costs balanced exactly across all the properties? How much money should a player receive for passing Go?

This is where the designer has to make the hard yards,

depth and soul. Being imaginative in your sources of research is also important. Hilariously, we ended up entertaining Kiev's professor of sociology for dinner in an attempt to enlist his help.

Equally bizarre was the Soviet library we found in Brixton. Going by the vaguely sinister name of The Society for Anglo-Soviet Co-operation, it's a vast library of Russian books tucked away in dilapidated house in the roughest part of Brixton. Naturally our man convinced himself he'd found a den of spies and that they thought he was an undercover MI6 agent. I think he'd been playing too many games.

Another key design responsibility is the interface – one

'Joe spent the first two months of the development in the British Library reading about the former Soviet Union – to generate enough information to create a living, breathing country that was to all intents real'

design document, which is usually just a couple of pages long and outlines the key points of the game. You then have to persuade your team and your publisher that's it's going to be the game of the decade.

You want the original vision to be inspirational enough to keep you going through the long months of development, and ambitious enough not to limit the team's creativity.

A great game is the culmination of a great initial concept and then thousands of smaller but perfectly formed creative ideas. It's also the work of people who are making a game they desperately want to play.

After the initial stage there are two important jobs a designer does. The first is to generate content for the game. The second is mechanical and involves creating the rules and subsystems that make the game work.

The content side of designing is, perhaps, the most fun. If we use Monopoly as an example, the content part of the job would entail naming the streets, creating Community Chest and Chance cards and choosing the style of the playing pieces ("I know, one player can be a boot and

often through the numbing grind of tweaking thousands of variables ("Hmm, yes, the axe is definitely a four-and-a-half"). It's for good reason that Joe is affectionately known as Spreadsheet Man. Some games require more design work than others.

Republic: The Revolution is an enormous game and requires a lot of design for a number of reasons. Firstly, the minute a player tries to do something and can't is the minute he remembers he's playing a game. This game simulates an entire country – which means there's a lot of work to make sure this doesn't happen. Secondly, a game in the real world needs to be accurate, whereas a sci-fi or fantasy game doesn't. People notice and mind very much if you misrepresent the real world.

On the content side, Joe spent the first two months of the development in the British Library reading about the former Soviet Union. The idea was to generate enough information to help us create a living, breathing country that was to all intents real.

The fictional country of Novistrana features elements of Belorussia, Ukraine, Azerbaijan and Abkhazia among others. Getting to this point involved hours of poring over books with fascinating titles such as 'Central Asia and The Caucasus after the Soviet Union'.

The fact that the player may never discover that the country's main crops are barley and buckwheat, or that 6.25 per cent of the population works in machinery production, isn't the point.

If a player only sees two per cent of everything we've put in, this implies that the other 98 per cent is present and correct. This reinforces the illusion of reality. These little details give a game its

of the purest tests of design skill. We have a principle here called the parent test, the ultimate challenge. This involves sitting one of our parents down in front of a game and seeing if they can pick it up within ten minutes. It's a pretty stringent test.

Other than imagination and creativity there are other skills that help you become a decent designer. An encyclopedic knowledge of games is extremely useful. If you ever see an interview with Scorsese or Tarantino you realise they spend their lives watching and studying films. A game designer should have the same dedication.

Being able to communicate your ideas, in conversation and on paper, is critical. Telling an artist that you want a Russian-looking building isn't very helpful; being able to show visual reference and explain your thinking is.

An analytical mind is also helpful. Lots of people play games. Few can explain what makes one better then the other. *TA* versus *Starcraft* anyone? If you can take a step back and isolate key strengths and failings it will help you with your own game.

It will also lend credence to your views, whereas telling a programmer to implement a feature because it's "good" won't. Perhaps most importantly you need good taste and intuition for what is cool and what plays well.

There is no secret to game design. Much of the magic of gameplay comes from the thousands of hours you invest in playing your own game. You'd be amazed at how many developers don't actually play their own game – incredible but true.

Another danger is that people can be precious with ideas. The right idea is the one that works best. This is why active discussion involving the whole team is so beneficial to the design process.

Finally, the most important thing is to keep focused on the single objective: fun. Games are games. Technology is cool but gameplay is always king.

Spreadsheet Man Joe McDonagh shares his vision. Pillow, anyone?

whitespace studio

Do you have designs on New Media?

We will give you comprehensive first hand experience working with cutting edge technology to create imaginative and innovative pieces of work at industry standards, giving you an invaluable tool for gaining access to the industry.

Year long full time courses starting in January: Animation, Interactive Design, Design for Film and Television, Shorts for Television

Short courses in Digital modelling, 3D Animation: beginning and intermediate 3D Studio Max, Web Design: Dreamweaver, Flash,

Photoshop, Director, Media 100, Premiere.

Small classes or individual courses tailored to your specific career or company needs.

If you are excited about moving image… are ambitious and creative… have an arts or IT background and the drive to succeed…

Then we want to hear from you.

Whitespace Studio
Tel: 0181 547 7066
E-mail: d.lawson@kingston.ac.uk

Where digital technology and creativity converge

Whitespace Studio at Kingston University is now offering courses for those of you who really want to get to grips with the digital world.

KINGSTON UNIVERSITY

 # Want to get into Games, Animation or Television?

Announcing a new Government sponsored training and research facility in the centre of London to get people into the Games and TV industries. This is an initiative to bring new talent into the industry and is supported by the DfEE, top facilities houses and hardware/software manufacturers.

We are launching in January

More details?
Ask for information on "The Finishing School"
CREATEC, Ealing Studios, Ealing Green, London W5 5EP Tel/fax: 0181 758 8619
courses@nfts-createc.org.uk

3D Animation ✪ 3D Studio Max ✪ Maya for Beginners and Advanced ✪ SoftImage Beginners and Advanced ✪ Designing for Virtual Sets ✪ and more
Digital Compositing and Effects ✪ Avid Media Illusion ✪ Quantel Editbox ✪ Quantel Henry ✪ After FX 4.0 ✪ Premiere 5 ✪ Avid Digital Studio ✪ Discreet Logic Effect ✪ Discreet Logic Flame ✪ Discreet Logic Edit ✪ and more
2D Animation ✪ Toonz ✪ Flash ✪ Animo ✪ and more

National
Film
Television
School

D/EE

CREATEC

metro new media

DO YOU WANT TO PLAY... OR BE A PLAYER?

ACCREDITED 3D STUDIO MAX TRAINING FOR GAMERS WHO WANT TO MOVE ONTO THE NEXT LEVEL

3 DAY INTENSIVE COURSES £330 + VAT

T: 0171 729 9992 F: 0171 739 7742
E: info@mnm.co.uk

35 KINGSLAND ROAD SHOREDITCH LONDON E2 8AA
www.mnm.co.uk

The UK's **best** technology magazine...

...now online

www.t3.co.uk

CLASSIFIED TO ADVERTISE CALL GLYN HUGHES ON 020 7317 2645 OR EMAIL glyn.hughes@futurenet.co.uk

DREAM - interactive -

'The North West's No.1 for import, retro and official games and consoles'

PlayStation NINTENDO 64 NEO GEO Dreamcast

0151 336 7644

• Prices correct at time of going to press • Strictly mail order prices only, shop retail prices will differ from advert prices • All above subject to availability • We reserve the right to to alter prices without notice • Opening hours: Monday to Friday 10.00am - 5.30pm and Sunday 10.00am - 1.00pm • *Free delivery on all games within the UK not next day guaranteed • A minimal charge will be made on most items •

VIDEO GAME CENTRE

We have a huge range of new & used video games, accessories, game related toys & hardware including many imports from Japan & U.S.A.

JAP DREAMCAST		JAP DREAMCAST SALE		OTHER INTERESTING STUFF	
Shenmue	£64.99	Giant Gram Wrestling	£35.00	Resident Evil 2 (N64 US)	
Virtua Striker 2000	£49.99	Climax Landers	£30.00	Pokemon gold/silver (GBC) + oads	
Zombie Revenge	£49.99	Super Speed Racing	£20.00	of Pokemon toys!	
Chu Chu Rocket	£34.99	Monaco GP2	£20.00	DC VGA box	£29.99
F1 World Championship	£49.99	Marvel v Capcom	£25.00	DC coloured joypads	
Resident Evil 2	£49.99	Tokyo Highway	£30.00	DC 6 button joypads	
Golf	£39.99	Streetfighter Zero 3	£30.00	Neo pocket (new style)	
Bangioh	£49.99	Cool Boarders	£35.00	NGP - Sonic	
Virtual on 2	£49.99	Blue Stinger (used)	£20.00	NGP JNK v Capcom	
Streetfighter 3	£49.99	Virtua Fighter 3	£30.00	PS Granturismo 2 (Jap)	
Giganing	£49.99	Redline Racer	£30.00	PS-Final fantasy Anthology	
Jojo Bizarre Adv.	£49.99	Toukon Retsuden 4	£30.00	PS - Grandia	
Star Gladiator 2	£49.99	Sega Rally 2	£35.00	Sat - Final Fantasy Fight Revenge	
Beserk	£49.99	Tetris 4D	£25.00	Sat - Streetfighter Zero III	
7 playable demo disk	£12.99	Air Force Delta (used)	£25.00	DC Crazy Taxi 27th Jan	

VISA 870 Wimborne Road, Bournemouth BH9 2DR Tel: 01202 527314

LivDigital
DVD VIDEO | VIDEO CD

Specialising in DVD and VCD
PO Box 6064 Nottingham NG5 3DF

DVD Players
ALL REGION DVD PLAYERS
Sony DVP-M35.............£389.99
JVC XV-K503TN (DTS)....£404.99
Samsung DVD808K........£229.99
Pioneer Dv505..............£299.99

DVD Movies
US DVD movies in stock.
Call for latest releases
Prices from £14.99

VCD Players
Panasonic SV-LP30......£134.99
Kebao VCD -M28.........£129.99
PSX VCD Card.............£34.99

VCD Movies
Call for latest releases
Also available HK Action VCDs

Dreamcast
NTSC Dreamcast & games in stock
Call for lastest price.

Import & Mail Order

Tel: 0115 9524119
Fax: 0115 9568820
email : mail@livdigital.co.uk
http ://www.livdigital.co.uk

TOTAL SOFTWARE UK LTD

    GAME BOY

The Fastest Growing Mail Order and Online Business

Many of our product prices are down this week - below trade price
We also sell Educational Software

SALES LINE: 0800 783 0395
Open Hours: 9am-9pm (Mon-Fri) 10am-6pm (Sat)

FREE DELIVERY
WE ACCEPT MAJOR CREDIT CARDS
VISIT OUR SECURE ONLINE SITE @ www.totalsoftware.co.uk

Games 2000

QUICK AND EASY MAIL ORDER SERVICE

DREAMCAST & ONE GAME
£220

Special Millennium Offer
All Games bought before 2000 under £30

CHEAPEST PRICES AROUND

VMU £16 With any Order

Race Control Wheel £39.99 With Any Order

PLAYSTATION & ANY GAME
£110

ORDER HOTLINE
0181 981 4555

We also stock:
Gameboy Color, Pokemon, N64 & PlayStation Conversions. Japanese Dreamcast £199 plays UK, US & Japanese Games.

9-10 College Terrace, London E3 5AN
Fax: 0181 981 4052

DREAM-TEK
01782 878805

ALL DREAMCAST JAP TITLES £39.99!!	ALL USA PLAYSTATION TITLES £38.99!!	ALL NINTENDO 64 USA TITLES £42.99!!
INC. ZOMBIE REVENGE ETC	INC. TOMB RAIDER 4 ETC	INC. RAGE WARS ETC

NEED WE SAY MORE??!!
SHIPPED DIRECT FROM OUR OFFICE IN THE USA USING INSURED, REGISTERED POST TO YOUR DOOR IN 3 OR 4 DAYS. IF YOU WANT TO KNOW MORE, GIVE US A CALL.

"USA DREAMCAST CONSOLE £199.99!!"
ALL USA DREAMCAST TITLES £39.99
DREAMCAST CONVERSIONS £36 INC 12 MONTHS WARRANTY!!

WE STOCK OVER 200 MUSIC CD'S AT THE UK'S BEST PRICES - AND ALL OURS ARE ORIGINAL NOT FAKES LIKE OUR LOCAL COMPETITORS.

DELTA VISA SWITCH MasterCard DREAM-TEK, 1A PITGREEN LANE, NEWCASTLE UNDER LYME, NORTH STAFFS ST5 0DQ OPENING HOURS: 10AM-5.30PM MON-SAT EMAIL: DREAMTEK41@HOTMAIL.COM

CYBER NET
Video Games Experts

The Best Mail Order Games on the Internet

Tel : 0181-789 7196
MAIL ORDER!

287 PUTNEY BRIDGE ROAD
LONDON SW15 2PT

Opening Hours
11am to 11pm Monday to Sunday

Visit our web site at : www.cybernet-filmstudio.com

Special Offer!
Buy Any Game and Get 2nd for Half Price
Only one coupon per person, valid till end of December 1999. Coupon must be presented at purchase of game.

CONSOLE CORNER
Import & UK Mail Order Games & DVDs

DC Console UK..................£189.99	Most UK Dreamcast Titles...........£32.99
DC Console US (inc. stepdown)...£189.99	Most US/JAP Dreamcast Titles........£39.99
Pre-order PS2 now, £25 deposit secures!	Most UK PlayStation Titles..........£28.99
Samsung DVD709 Multi Region ...£249.99	Most US N64 Titles.................£44.99
Console Accessories..............£BEST	**LATEST RELEASES:**
NEO-GEO Pocket Colour JAP	Soul Calibur DC UK................£32.99
(English Menus/Universal) £49.99	Shenmue DC JAP...................£49.99
	D2 DC JAP........................£44.99
	Virtua Striker DC JAP............£39.99
	Resident Evil 2 DC JAP...........£39.99
	Tomb Raider 4 PSX .UK..£28.99 US..£36.99
	Resident Evil 3 PSX US...........£39.99

MasterCard Tel: 01724 855155 VISA
Hours of business: 9am-7pm Mon-Fri, 9am-6pm Sat
Website: www.consolecorner.com

BE AWARE: CHIPPING VOIDS ANY SONY UK WARRANTY ON YOUR PLAYSTATION. PROCEED AT YOUR OWN RISK

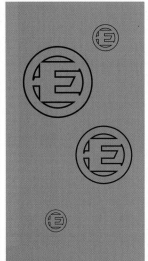

INDIANA JONES AND THE TEMPLE OF DOOM

As George Lucas' whip-snarling, wise-cracking hero leaps into the realms of PC 3D gaming, **Edge** looks back at a game which used altogether less capable tools in order to give gamers a taste of peril-strewn adventures against an evil cult

Classic late-'80s Atari coin-op presentation at work (top). Typically of the day, the difficulty-select screen (above) showed the sort of imagination Atari could muster

L ike fruit-shaped power-ups and end-of-level bosses bearing suspiciously exposed areas of vulnerability, the mine-cart level has long been a staple component of videogame design. From *Donkey Kong Country* to its recent polygonal 64bit successor, its inclusion has often seemed token at best, thrown in by the developer to alleviate any symptoms of boredom with the action proper. However, if ever a game were to be forgiven using such an obvious gameplay mechanic it must surely be 1985's *Indiana Jones And The Temple Of Doom*: the mine-cart scene of the source movie was a pivotal point, and to ignore its potential in videogame form would have been borderline sacrilege.

But the game did not work simply by hauling over such obvious concepts to Atari's 16bit coin-op technology of the day. True, it offered nothing revolutionary in gameplay terms – indeed, the three-quarter-viewed action often felt disparagingly fuzzy, the player blundering around some loose-feeling, essentially platform-based levels – but the audio accompaniment evoked the movie's score with dramatic effect, leaving any major gameplay misgivings to fall by the wayside. In the right environment (ie, an arcade whose operator didn't skimp on volume levels), *Temple Of Doom* proved to be the most movie-like coin-op gaming experience since *Star Wars* arrived two years earlier.

It's no good attempting to appreciate *Temple Of Doom*'s charm via emulation. Track it down in the right arcade, though, and, among the cigarette and Coke stains, you may appreciate its value.

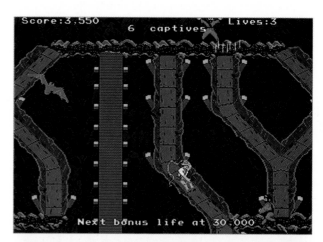

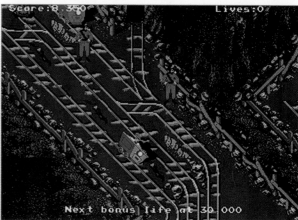

In its day, *Temple Of Doom* was one of the most graphically advanced bitmapped creations to hit the coin-op scene, utilising Atari's super-crisp display technology. The level of detail available allowed artists to create levels which rarely failed to serve justice to key elements of the movie

From left to right: the crux of the gameplay broke few bounds; mine-carting in its rightful place; baldie Mola Ram makes his presence felt; complex scripting indeed

| Manufacturer: Atari | 1985 | Developer: In-house | Coin-op/various |

EDGEVIEW

The videogame world never stands still, riding the breaking wave of advancing technology. In this regular column **Edge** puts the industry's progress in perspective with a look at yesteryear's headlines: five years ago this month

Edge issue 17, February 1994

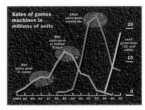

As the 16bit decline fully kicked in, issue 17 plotted new hardware sales. Fascinating

I t had never happened this way before. No two major formats had ever launched alongside each other. In some respects, they shouldn't have. But **Edge** took delivery of new machines from both Sony and Sega in December 1994, paving the way for the systems' flagship titles to be pitched head to head in the reviews section of the February issue. And it was of little surprise, having monitored the development of both PlayStation *Ridge Racer* and Saturn *Virtua Fighter* over many months prior to their release, that both were of sterling quality.

But what was on the cover of this landmark issue? Clue: it didn't bear a Sega badge. Why? Because, even at this early stage, it was clear that the industry was gagging for what Sony proposed to bring to the party. With *Ridge Racer* Namco provided ample evidence of what could be achieved on the format given even limited development time (it was pieced together in around six months), and this was a spark to the blue touchpaper. Once Sega's hardware limitations became evident, few developers sat on the fence.

Looking back at issue 17, little else is of note. Simply put, the revolution started here. **E**

Clockwise from top left: Nintendo's venture into 32bit territory gets an auspicious welcome in Edge; Sony's first piece of console hardware finds rather more favour; PlayStation *Ridge Racer*; Saturn *Virtua Fighter*

Did they really say that?

ATD's **Martin Green**: "The one thing Atari have been very good at is saying, 'We want the best product.'" Wanting is one thing…

Did Edge really say that?

'On the Saturn, [*Virtua Fighter*] will make many people stop, look at their bank balance and then fork out for Sega's new machine.' But not *that* many, apparently

Testscreens (and ratings)

Ridge Racer (PS; 9/10), *Virtua Fighter* (Saturn; 9/10), *Transport Tycoon* (PC; 8/10), *Rise of the Robots* (PC; 2/10), *KOF '94* (8/10; Neo-Geo), *Creature Shock* (6/10; PC), *SSFII X* (3DO; 8/10), *Samurai Shodown* (Neo-Geo; 7/10)

PIXELPERFECT

Every gamer has occasional moments of sparkling excitement, be it the first time *Speedball* booted up, or completing *Sabrewulf*. Here, Curly Monsters' MD **Nick Burcombe** explains his admiration for a game that pressed every button

D id it all start with the Atari 2600 and *Combat* or *Dig Dug*? The great grandfather of all firstperson shooters – 3D *Monster Maze* on the ZX81? The crappy seaside arcades of Southport with *Tempest* and *Mr Do*?

If I had to talk about just one game that pushed all the right buttons it would have to be *Elite* on the BBC B (disc version). *Elite* was of a scale and depth nobody had seen in those days (rarely captured these days, some would say).

Its packaging, manual, novella, the 3D graphics, and the size of its universe were remarkable. For me, it really was the complete package. I still remember

some great moments. Making my first profit (a breakthrough when you consider how hard it was to dock); buying my first beam laser; chasing the stolen research military ship – the Constrictor – halfway across the universe, and, of course, eventually mastering recklessly fast manual docking.

People have tried to create this experience again. Perhaps they will. So far all the game efforts I've played have over complicated and lost the essence of the lone trader. I used to love the fact that I was in control of my little part of the *Elite* universe. How I went about seemed entirely up to me. A gameplay rarity indeed. **E**

Vector graphics drove the game that drove the man to tobacco. Braben and Bell surely have a lot to answer for

Take me to your dancing queen

Japan: Following the success of *Seaman*, Sega took to the streets of Shibuya to promote its dancing and shooting rhythm game, *Space Channel 5*. Sega is hoping it will appeal to the fabled hordes of 'light users' that it needs to attract to make Dreamcast a hit in Japan. Sega's executives turned out to have their photos taken with a human representation of the game's heroine Ulala, and its producer Tetsuya Mizuguchi. Held in front of the Shibuya's main train station, three giant screens on the new Q-Front tower displayed the game as Mizuguchi-san demonstrated it in action, drawing a large crowd in the process. Because even here, a bunch of brightly coloured aliens cutting a rug isn't the kind of thing you see every day of the week.

(Left) Sega president Shoichiro Irimajiri is flanked by *Space Channel 5* producer Tetsuya Mizuguchi and its star, Ulala

Introducing the new BFG (big foam gun)

US: As if anyone really doubted that the firstperson shooter is the ubiquitous computer game, the release of *Nerf ArenaBlast* is the final proof. A bizarre mixture of the *Unreal* engine and the Nerf foam gun franchise, it's Hasbro's way of showing some hardcore potential while keeping the action clean for the kids.

Three different game modes are available. The most obvious is PointMatch, which is a take on the traditional deathmatch, although it doesn't actually involve frags. Instead, points are given out for shooting an opponent and the higher ranked they are the more points are awarded. Using a less powerful gun results in higher scores too.

Arena Race is a mad rush to be the first player to run through seven flags. Death results in respawning at the last flag passed. There's also Scavenger Hunt, which involves shooting balls into targets.

The most unusual thing about the whole exercise is how surreal it is to play. There are no shadows to hide in and without the blood splats or gibs of the real deal there's little feedback to tell you whether you are actually hitting someone. It's akin to playing *Quake* with cottonwool in your brain – but that was surely Hasbro's intention.

It could be titled 'Unreal: The Toy Shop' – *Nerf BlastArena* is garish, foamy fun for kids

Battleship goes online

UK: A launch party with a difference followed the merger of Wireplay and ICE and the subsequent successful stock market float. The online gaming and retail site Gameplay.com hired HMS Belfast on London's Thames. And while free beer, multiplayer *Sega Rally* and *Unreal Tournament*, and top DJs drew an expectant crowd of freeloaders, by the time **Edge** arrived the ship was packed, the bar was close to dry, and all the canapés had been scoffed. At least solace could be sought among a small group of coders fervently discussing infinite monkey engines.

Sticking to your guns

Japan: The Dreamcast release of mecha blaster *Virtual On* also sees the debut of a twin stick controller and, more importantly, a VS cable, allowing two consoles to be connected together – the only way to truly appreciate the game.

(Top right) Gameplay chairman Mark Strachan donned a uniform and ensured everything on the Belfast was shipshape. (Apart from beer)

Released with *Virtual On*: the twin stick (¥5800/approx. £35) and VS cable (¥300/£18)

Superheroes skin up

Captain America, Spider-Man and the Borg – just some of the skins that could be appearing soon on a *Unreal Tournament* server near you

US: It may not be viewed with the same seriousness among online communities as mods and level design, but there's something far more appealing and playful about customised character skin. A recent trend is superhero skins for *Unreal Tournament*, with characters from the Marvel comics such as Captain America, The Incredible Hulk and Spider-Man being particularly popular. For further details, visit **www.unreality.org/painful detail/** where would-be designers can download complete skin sets, check out the skins of the week and even some of Epic's character grid maps, to ensure that the textures join in the right places. And then try to build Juggernaut.

(out there) REPORTAGE

Revealed: biggest joystick in the world

UK: If bringing the arcade into the home is purely a matter of size, then Blaze's PlayStation Twin Joystick is one to watch. Five times bigger than the console it plugs into, the monster peripheral has all the usual buttons. The question is, do you have enough floor space for it?

And the cost of twoplayer arcade heaven? A meagre £40

Seaman comes to all ye faithful

Japan: Developer Vivarium recently took the concept behind one of the most innovative games of recent times one step further with a limited-edition *Seaman* Christmas card service. Providing the recipient was in possession of a special GD-ROM, users were able to give their Seaman a festive greeting using the game's microphone and Dreamcast's Internet connection, sending the appropriately attired hybrid to pass the message in time for the festive season. The recipient could then give Seaman a reply. Bearing in mind the service's expiry date is December 25, maybe Sega is planning an Easter bunny version for 2000.

The complete 'send and reply' Christmas Seaman package cost ¥3,780 (£23)

Calculating Lara Croft

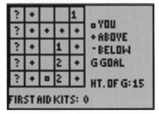 

TI-82 *Tomb Raider*: more fun than typing '58008' and turning the screen upside down

UK: With Core announcing the introduction of the *Tomb Raider* series to the Game Boy Color, it's instructive to look back to Lara's first adventure on a handheld. Even before *Tomb Raider III* was released, Chris Edwards had attempted his own version of the daredevil heroine on the Texas Instruments TI-82 graphing calculator.

Featuring full 3D movement, five levels and five different enemies, the TI-82 version may not have won any awards for prettiness but it certainly demonstrated the kind of devotion that would see *The Last Revelation* topping the Christmas charts.

Boy exposes thermal underground

US: Ostensibly the result of being stuck in a foreign country without a darkroom for developing black-and-white pictures, the Game Boy Camera website is at the hub of exhibitions demonstrating the prowess of the handheld's digital camera and thermal printer. Most impressive is Airstrike, a selection of 'apocalyptic images of American suburbs'. There is even a tutorial discussing the best ways to frame and contrast images. Apparently, best results can be attained by tilting the camera and getting in close to the subject. For more details visit **www.tapir.org/gbc**

From images of moody grunge rockers to would-be Ronald McDonalds and beady-eyed ostriches, the Game Boy Camera is catching it all

Legends hit the small screen

Japan: 2000 is the year that portable consoles will grow up. Not only are Nintendo and SNK preparing their next-generation 32bit systems, but the likes of Solid Snake and Sonic are making the jump.

Metal Gear Ghost Babel takes the basic scenario of the original MSX game. The goal remains – to fight through the 13 levels to destroy Metal Gear. Similarly *Sonic Pocket Adventure* on the Neo-Geo Pocket Color appears to rely heavily on its previous Mega Drive incarnation. Studio 3's classic 8bit *IK+* (International Karate Plus) is also receiving the handheld treatment – crossing over to the Game Boy Color, while exploring its technical limitations with its large character sprites.

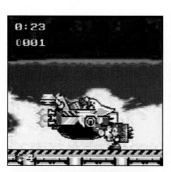

Soon to be playable in trains, planes and buses around the world (from left): *Sonic Pocket Adventure*, *IK+*, and *Metal Gear Ghost Babel*

Level driving field

UK: According to Logic3, one of the biggest problems in gaming today is what to do with your steering wheel when there's no convenient coffee table in reach.

While it's not something that has ever hampered **Edge**'s gaming, those who do feel the need will be able to satisfy their urge with the TopDrive Podium. It's only £17 and you can put hot cups of tea on it, too.

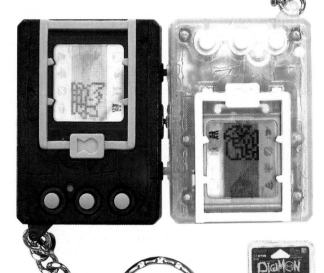

Digimon: the new breed

UK: Heralding the latest round of Bandai's social fighting pets comes *Digimon 2*, offering 14 different creatures. Each must be nurtured from hatchling to rookie and then champion before a final evolution into the ultimate fighting beast.

Each day it will demand attention, food, vitamins, training, its toilet flushing, medical attention, and the light turned out when it falls asleep. The reason behind all this pampering is that the wee beast loves to fight its fellow Digimons, which it does via the ingenious connector sockets on top of its casing.

Edge has five pairs of *Digimon 2*s to give away. For a chance to win, all you have to do is send in the names you would give your pair of virtual pets – the most imaginative examples win. Send your entries with your name and address to Edge Digimon 2 Competition, 30 Monmouth Street, Bath, BA1 2BW, before January 22. Usual **Edge** competition rules apply.

DataStream

Rise in Sega stock following the announcement that the release of *Shenmue* was being brought forward to December 29: **5 per cent**
Number of games that have been played on Blizzard's online game hub Battle.net: **45m**
Time on Battle.net that is spent in chat rooms: **25 per cent**
Japanese households in possession of a PC: **20 per cent**
Number of US homes with at least one console: **37m**
Number of copies of *Ridge Racer V* and *Tekken Tag Tournament* Namco expects to ship at PlayStation2's launch: **750,000**
Number of PlayStation2 titles Square will release in 2000: **10**
Number of PlayStation2 consoles Merrill Lynch expects Sony to sell between March 2000 and March 2004: **100m**
Number of Dreamcasts Sega hopes to sell in 2000: **10m**
Total predicted net loss for Sega for FY'99: **$104m**
Amount of royalties GT paid to Reflections during its last financial quarter following the success of *Driver*: **$7.5m**
Year that Datamonitor predicts the number of console gamers playing online will surpass the number of PC gamers playing online: **2003**
Number of hits on Burger King's *Pokémon* tied-in Web site during its first six hours live: **1.3m**
Number of weeks it took Sega to sell 1m Dreamcasts in America: **11**
Number of Sidewinder Force Feedback Pro joysticks Microsoft has sold: **1m**

Welcome to the scary seats

Japan: Forget about the ghost train – the most frightening theme park ride looks set to be *Biohazard 4D Terror*. Created by Capcom, theme park movie specialist Digital Amuse, and special effects company VLM, it will use special dynamic seating as well as 3D glasses. The seats will move and vibrate, and Digital Amuse intends to increase the overall atmosphere of the 15-minute ride by blowing air and water over the audience.

The scenario will use a cannibalised version of *Bio Hazard 3*, although it is expected that some extra scenes will be added. The first ride will be finished in June. Initially, ten will be located in Japan. Plans for bringing the ride to America and Europe will be announced soon. Hold on to your potatoes…

The attraction is being overseen by Yasushisa Imakawa of *Space Griffon* fame, and Capcom's Shinji Hikuchi

They may look comfortable enough, but these seats could be a portal to zombie-driven terror

BECK
Midnite Vultures
(Geffen)

Rock's urban magpie is back with a fresh beak of shiny catchy tunes that just happened to catch his eye. But after the lazy folk hip-hop of 'Mutations', this new collection is ready to swing. From the cover artwork to single 'Sexx Laws' and the Prince clone, orgasmic falsetto of 'Debra', Beck is ready to party like it's, well, time to party. Scratch the metallic paint from the surface and the simple man-boy the girls fell in love with when he sang 'Loser' remains. Only this time, he's wiggling his hips in tight pink PVC pants.

VARIOUS ARTISTS
Pop Tics
(Bungalow)

A total of 17 pop songs, each under two minutes long, makes up the musical side of this collection – although there's much more in the package. Each artist has submitted an image for the accompanying 70-page liner note/book and a gimmick for the website (www.poptics.com). And the best thing about it? Without question it's Doktor Kosmos & Sweden Graphics' track 'No One At Home' – replete with its novel use of doorbells as a melodic instrument.

DIVINE STYLER
Word Power 2
(Mo' Wax)

Few scenes are more convoluted than hip-hop – sometimes it seems to be a revolving door between jail, hospital and the morgue. It's a fact not lost on Divine Styler who, over the last ten years, has experienced both critical acclaim with the Rhyme Syndicate, spent several spells in correctional facilities and turned to Islam. It's this latter move which dominates Word Power 2. It's rap from the muezzin: a call to prayer.

Author: **Arthur C Clarke**
Publisher: **Victor Gollancz**
ISBN: **0575 06790X**

Author: **Steve Beard**
Publisher: **Codex**
ISBN: **1 899598 12 X**

PROFILES OF THE FUTURE

Few 20th Century writers have had the influence of Arthur C Clarke. From geostationary satellites to space travel, he has consistently managed to find the hidden potential in already existing technology. He obviously isn't infallible, though, which makes *Profile of the Future* an all the more interesting read.

Consisting of essays written for Playboy in 1961-2, the collection covers a multitude of subjects from events that were then still to occur, such as the moon landing, to things that would still be considered flights of fancy – the control of gravity and time travel for example. However, as Clarke himself cautions: 'The only way of finding the limits of the possible is by going beyond them into the impossible.'

Like all good science-fiction writers, his skill is to make outrageous statements seem almost normal, thanks to the judicious application of scientific thinking and an easy writing style. A good example is the chapter on invisibility. After quickly dismissing the traditional view of the invisible man (the reactions of life depend on cells not being transparent to light), he then effortlessly segues into an investigation of the possibilities of time travel.

Not all the essays are so fanciful, though. Clarke has always had a taste for the mechanical and there are discussions concerning still emerging earthbound technologies such as ground effort craft. But he is at his best when talking about terraforming the other planets in the solar system – a project currently undergoing official evaluation – and the problems of communication in deep space travel.

DIGITAL LEATHERETTE

After a steady stream of UK cyberpunk texts last year, 1999 was a barren time for those who like their alternative futures set in the gritty remnants of downtown Canary Wharf. It's a place that *i-D* technology columnist Steve Beard knows well. His self-styled 'ethno-techno London cypherpunk novel' twists the big city's streets into a patchwork tale of Blakeian mysticism and informational intrigue.

But *Digital Leatherette* is not an easy text. Written in single chapter blocks with little obvious relationship to those before and after, it's something of a mind-freak.

Unrelated characters, events and magic are thrown up, building an atmosphere which is as much to do with the absence of a complete story as the fragments actually provided. But any book that can attempt to suggest links between the English nationalism of Morrissey and the cabbalism of Elizabethan alchemists such as John Dee must be saying something. The question is, what?

INTERNET
Site: Pokémon Must Be Destroyed
URL: www.mustbedestroyed.com

For every million under-eights who go to bed clutching a cuddly Pikachu, there's a bad-tempered 30-something who can't stand the sight of the little things – and this is their Web site. It's possible to vote for the next method of execution, whether that is having their heads mashed with a sledge hammer or simply being thrown into a microwave. You can then download the resulting movie. Despite **Edge**'s love of 'Bulbasi' (once a Bulbasaur, now a Venusaur), there is something admirable about the sheer devotion of these people to their chosen cause. They've even managed to rope legendary Hong Kong action movie star Samo Hung into the action, who duly breaks a plank with Pikachu stapled to its centre.

VIEWPOINT

EXPRESS YOURSELF IN **EDGE** – WRITE TO: LETTERS, **EDGE**, 30 MONMOUTH STREET, BATH BA1 2BW (email: edge@futurenet.co.uk)

The PlayStation 2 coverage in many magazines hints at far too many sequels.

In the NGPS *FIFA* games, apart from making every blade of grass fully rendered and able to move to authentic weather effects, what can be done to stop the game becoming dull?

I think football rules will have to change to innovate EA's *FIFA* licence. It apes the game so closely and with such little imagination that I don't believe Sony can realistically charge the full price for a new game (new *FIFA* games for the PC should be free patch downloads).

I also see new a *Tekken* game which claims to have graphical effects as good as the intro in *Tekken 3*. Why? There is no reason to do this, it won't further the genre (unless it has groundbreaking new physics). Meanwhile I see that *Gran Turismo* is getting a sequel for both PlayStations, with more cars and prettier graphics.

I am a very sore ex-Saturn owner, and if I don't see some groundbreaking new ideas on the NGPS, I will hope that Bill Gates squashes Sony under his immense wallet and his new X-Box console!

**Iain Cousins,
via email**

Your Console War II article (**E**79) makes rather an important point that you touched upon only briefly – developers have the power.

As much as Sony would like to have the software market wrapped around its little finger, it surely knows that this position of power is, in a sense, transparent. Without the support of its countless legions of thirdparty software

developers it would be sunk.

Nintendo's decision to stick with cartridges has dealt a blow to the company's image in some people's eyes, but I strongly admire its purist stance and hope that developers

will give it a second chance.

After all, Rare has delivered first-class software for the N64 ever since it began and, to a certain extent, so has Acclaim. It will be software, not hardware, that wins or

unashamedly fuel Sony's over-inflated corporate ego.

If you are going to make predictions, you need to establish whether your stance is quality software or marketing success.

'To make games which rival films and books, the way forward is to **find decent gameplay, then focus** on the characters and plot instead of photorealistic **graphics'**

Are you a creative magazine or a business magazine?

'But is it art?' (**E**79) makes it obvious that because interactive entertainment is mainstream developers are always ruled in some

What will *FIFA* bring to the next generation? Not a great deal, reckons Iain Cousins

loses this battle. Developers would be well advised to wield their power carefully and not be swayed by a seductive company whispering sweet nothings into their ears.

Also, how do you measure success? You credit Nintendo as having the best in-house development talent (Shigeru Miyamoto) but then you

way by public acceptance, and many wild, brave experiments fail because we are not willing to accept them (although it is more often because they are simply unplayable, and not merely misunderstood).

An analogy can be drawn with Igor Stravinski's 'Rite of Spring', which caused a riot

when it was first performed.

Regarding finger-pointing at Sony (Viewpoint, **E**79), I personally fully agree with Ashley Simmons.

If Sony wants to be an omnipotent giant it has to accept persecution as an occupational hazard. Microsoft is the perfect example of this. Because of its unprecedented success in the PC market it has been branded a monopoly. Many people fear Bill Gates' plans for world domination. It's fun to see Sony being taken down a peg or two.

**James Slater,
via email**

Edge's stance concerning the next round of hardware wars is neither quality software nor marketing success, it encapsulates everything. And the big picture spells out the favourite in large letters.

If Sega and Dreamcast will have a hard time with Joe Average, then Sony and PlayStation2 will too (Console War II, **E**79).

Joe will walk into a high street shop and see the first PlayStation for £60 offering more than 200 games on the shelf. Joe doesn't care about DVD or the network digital entertainment market. Joe wouldn't know a polygon if it bit him (let alone 16m of the things). Joe's happy with a Matsui video plugged into a Matsui TV bought on a package deal.

I'm happy playing *Soul Calibur* and sending emails on Dreamcast. I'm looking forward to the future of all the consoles, after all, it's meant to be fun. Just one question, is a casual gamer different to Joe? Now I've started something.

**Tim Surman,
via email**

The super-mass market has a phone at home; the mass market has a mobile phone as well as a land line. That's the distinction. Joe Average fits into the former category, casual gamers into the latter. Simple.

Edge readers continue to knock their heads together over the next generation and who's going to 'win' (**E**79).

But the videogames industry has moved on fundamentally since the 16bit days. Nick Ralph reckons the N64 was a failure. I guess many people do. But I doubt Nintendo lost money on the N64. And it has played host to some of the greatest videogames ever made. I've had an N64 for two years and I haven't run out of games to play.

Maybe it failed to live up to some people's expectations. Maybe Nintendo has made some bad decisions, but if you want to play *Zelda, Mario, Wave Race, 1080°, GoldenEye, Lylat Wars* and many more you have to have an N64.

It all smacks of numbers being our most important criteria of judgement. It is, to the companies (but not, I reckon, to Shigeru Miyamoto), but we are consumers. We want great games.

It may gall me that not everyone in the videogaming world has played *Lylat Wars* and realised that it is probably one of the best shoot 'em ups ever, but I can still play it whenever I like.

The classic argument (and **Edge** has bought into this one) is that if the platform doesn't sell enough, it will fold. Perhaps, in the past, but the industry is much bigger now.

The videogames market is exploding. Surely there will be enough room for everyone. Will

something like the N64 be a failure if it only sells a quarter of the volume of the PlayStation? *The Guardian* only has one tenth the sales of *The Sun,* and I don't consider *The Guardian* to be a failure.

There is some interesting speculation to be made about the next generation. Will each medium (Dreamcast: Internet, PS2: DVD) find a separate niche? Will more people have more than one console? Will all shops stock products for so many different consoles? Could one company become the industry standard on hardware? Sony missed out on Betamax, will it have its revenge with PS2/DVD?

In a market this big there's more to the next generation than numbers of sales.

Alex Rousso,
via email

Comparing newspaper sales to entertainment consumer electronics sales has no value whatsoever (one costs pence and is immediately disposable, the other costs pounds and is expected to stick around).

As you correctly note, the industry is bigger than it ever has been, and it's for precisely this reason that the near future could see one format emerging as the de facto standard. Sega is already developing software for Nintendo hardware. Maybe Sega PS2 games aren't so far off, either.

Your article about whether or not videogames are art (**E**79) was interesting and enjoyable. But it stated that films successfully contemplate themes such as love, loss, death and failure which *Half-Life* and every other game does not. I have three words for you: *Final Fantasy VII*, the most emotionally

charged game I have ever had the joy of playing. The Aeris death sequence conjures up more emotion than 'Titanic'.

I know videogames are not everybody's taste. I know people who would much rather read a good book. I think that to make games which rival films and books, the way forward is to find decent gameplay, then focus on the characters and plot instead of photorealistic graphics and the like.

It is the difference between a regular Channel 5 TV movie and 'Schindler's List'.

James Wardle,
via email

It is only a matter of time, surely, before developers realise the money to be made writing PC software is minimal compared to the leading consoles.

With piracy being rife and the hindering complications, cost and impracticality of PC gaming, I don't understand how it is still supported by many developers as a viable gaming format.

The Japanese are the finest developers on earth, yet few of

them choose to develop for the format. This leaves the PC with dull western sims, the usual genres that have now become saturated, and a few promising titles – most notably *Republic*. All this means people who choose the PC as their premier gaming format must be either slightly ignorant or very dedicated.

When even Microsoft realises that creating a console is needed to cater for gamers' needs, the argument is prematurely resolved.

Jonti Davies,
via email

It's an installed userbase issue. Never mind any other consideration: so long as PCs are moving from the shelves of PC World, PC games will continue to be made.

Sharing Danny Edgar's concerns (Viewpoint, **E**79), I emailed Sega to find out if *Soul Calibur* would include the 60Hz option. The reply, on October 27, was slightly different to that which Sega sent him: 'At the moment we don't know the exact specs of *Soul Calibur*, but contact us again in two weeks and we should be able to tell you'.

I put this down to Sega being reluctant to inform me that a 60Hz option would not be present after all. I could not believe that Sega just didn't know. This is the most anticipated game in Sega's lineup.

Most worryingly, I had to ask the question. Surely all the launch titles for Sega's console (the firstparty ones at least) should have supported this feature. I would have thought including the option to switch between the two frequencies would be much less troublesome than, say (God forbid), actually

'I don't understand how PC gaming is still supported by many developers as a viable gaming format. The Japanese are the finest developers, few of them choose the format'

optimising the PAL conversion to run at full screen/speed.

I find it hard to believe that Dreamcast software is selling so well that Sega can simply throw away European profits for the sake of a little extra effort.

James Wheeler,
via email

I don't understand the point of all these new next generation consoles from Sony and Nintendo. Why will someone spend (at least in the UK) £300-plus on something that will only play games and bad (without a MPEG2 decoder) DVD movies?

In Sony's case, you won't be able to surf the Net as standard, and in Nintendo's, you won't be able to watch DVD movies. Each time a company (with Sega in mind) announces its brand's spankingly brilliant specs, the PCs catch up with the technology by the time it is released.

Didn't we all wow at the first pictures of Tower Of Babylon on Dreamcast? We watched the best use of 3D yet. Now, a P300 with a Voodoo2 can manage it. Who will want to spend £250 on the PS2? A little gamer kid? A middle-aged businessman? How about some parents buying it for their kids?

The teenage gamer will invariably buy a Dreamcast for, at most, half the price. The middle-aged businessman will not find that a console (and games especially) appeals to him. The parents will buy a PC for educational purposes. I'm sure the PS2 will do well in Japan (where anything techy goes), but in the US/UK it doesn't appear to fit into any specific age category.

Too expensive to some, too limited to others. If you can afford it, shop around for a good £500 PC, if not, buy a Dreamcast. That gives you access to a huge library of games, you can surf and play on the Net and have large upgrade options.

Mad_Sk8er,
via email

Hey, rabid Dreamcast owners! Come up with a less convincing pro-Sega rant than this one and win a prize!

I get the feeling **Edge** is on the verge of disappearing up its own arse. This hardcore-gamer-versus-casual-gamer debate has gone far enough.

Just when we seem to be getting past the sad 'my machine is better than your machine' argument, we come up with the new 'I'm a hardcore gamer, you're just a casual one'. Who cares!

I have to agree with Mark Hall (**E**79). I've been playing videogames since I was 12. I admit I've probably bought at least five football, five beat 'em ups and five driving games over the last few years. I love a good football game, especially in twoplayer mode, but I also play plenty of obscure Jap import garbage.

Just before the release of the UK Dreamcast I traded in my Jap DC that I'd had since last November, at an extremely popular London-based import shop. They asked me why on Earth I would trade in a Jap DC over a UK one.

I thought this was easy to

answer, what with 60Hz options on most games, instant Internet access, the fact that *Shenmue* will be virtually unplayable on import, and in my opinion I think the best software will be mostly from Europe and the US (save for maybe *Giga Wing* more recently).

Leave this argument well alone in the future and let someone enjoy a game of *Ready 2 Rumble/FIFA* as much as the next person.

In the end all we want to do is play decent games, new or old genres. I'll bet that Lionhead will die if *Black & White* ends up appealing only to the so-called hardcore gamer. This is going to be a game that every player on the planet should be able to try.

Richard Jones,
via email

'On the verge'? 'On the verge'? Completely stuck up there, Rich.

So you can play *Soul Calibur* using the DC fishing rod controller. It may turn out to be another gimmicky option but here we have innovation that hasn't been seen for some time.

Early next year, Rare will release *Perfect Dark* which is compatible with the Game Boy camera so you

can see your mates on screen as you shoot them. Great. So what other areas of innovation are coming up? DVD players? Analogue controllers? Larger memory cards?

Perhaps there is a great deal of innovation within games without

unnecessary add-ons. But how about the following for some ideas:
1. Controllers with mini-jack in and out sockets so we can all wear headsets in deathmatches with our mates. The software could increase the voice volume the nearer you get to someone. Even without the microphone you could hear footsteps relative to where you are with the headphones. The same principle works in sports games.
2. A motion-sensor add-on for your controller. Imagine playing a firstperson shoot 'em up in which the angle you hold your controller moves the direction of a torch. If you had a Rumble Pak for scary moments the torchlight would be all over the place. Very scary.
3. Games where one player drives a car and the other uses the lightgun to shoot baddies.
4. A bonus game where player one has the gun and player two must run from one end of a field to the other without getting shot – like that game in 'Gladiators.'

We would like to see some crazy ideas being suggested amid the pressure of all this next-generation conflict. We are not satisfied with *RR4, Tekken 4, Tomb Raider 4*, and *GT2000*. We want something new.

Nathan Baseley,
via email

Try Taito's Lucky'n'Wild coin-op for a taster of how your third idea works.

In 'Console War II', you say Microsoft's strength is hardware, not software. Er, were you using buggy Microsoft software when you came up with this?

Adam Keith,
via email

Ah, a good old transpositional error. They're the best, aren't they?

'Who will want to spend £250 on the PS2? I'm sure it will do well in Japan **(where anything hi-tech goes),** but in the US/UK it doesn't appear to fit into any specific **age category'**

You are a UK developer with a new computer game, Web site or other application. You reckon it's the best. Want to focus world attention on it?

Enter the **Edge/Developers@Milia 2000 Competition** and you could win a trip to Cannes to showcase your project at the world's interactive content marketplace on February 15-18.

All you have to do to enter is return the completed entry form, with your project, by January 26 to the address detailed below. The competition is open only to UK developers who have not previously rented an exhibition booth at Milia. The winning individual or studio, selected by **Edge,** will be given:

■ A free counter desk at the Developer Village.
■ A free registration for the Milia 2000 exhibition
■ Round trip (air travel) to Cannes, France
■ Accommodation for three nights (February 15, 16 and 17).

Milia 2000 is supporting innovation and content development more than ever. It has launched Developers@Milia 2000 to gather Web designers, graphic artists, programmers and game developers from around the globe. It's an unprecedented place for networking and doing business with industry professionals, publishers and media.

Developers@Milia 2000 will include a Developer Village, conferences geared towards developers, networking services and events plus a package including accommodation.

For more information about Milia 2000, including details of the Think.Tank Summit which takes place on February 14-15, visit the Milia Web site (**www.milia.com**). For full competition rules, visit the **Edge** Web site (http://fnetedit1/edge) or request a copy from **Edge**'s office. A copy of the entry form is also available on the **Edge** Web site.

COMPETITION ENTRY FORM

To enter the competition, please complete, sign and return this form, or a copy of it, **before January 26**, to Edge Developers@Milia 2000 Competition, 30 Monmouth Street, Bath, BA1 2BW.

Applications must include a complete prototype of the project on CD-ROM, compatible with PC or Mac.

Project title: ....

Project type: (game/Web site/other): ....
....
....
....

Name: ....

Company: ....

Address: ....
....

Email: ....

Phone: .... Fax: ....

I wish to submit my project in the **Edge** Developers@Milia 2000 competition. I undertake to agree to the competition rules available on the **Edge** website, or on request from **Edge**'s office.

Date: ....

Signature: ....

THINK.TANK SUMMIT: FEBRUARY 14-15, 2000
EXHIBITION: FEBRUARY 15-18, 2000
PALAIS DES FESTIVALS: CANNES, FRANCE

NEXT MONTH:

THE ORIGINAL SURVIVAL HORROR RETURNS